HIS
Majesty
AND
MISSION

EDITED BY NICHOLAS J. FREDERICK
AND KEITH J. WILSON

RSC
BYU

DESERET
BOOK

Published by the Religious Studies Center, Brigham Young University, Provo, Utah, in cooperation with Deseret Book Company, Salt Lake City.

Visit us at rsc.byu.edu.

Printed in the United States of America by Sheridan Books, Inc.

DESERET BOOK is a registered trademark of Deseret Book Company.

Visit us at DeseretBook.com.

ISBN: 978-1-9443-9412-7
Retail US: $17.99

Cover and interior design by Madison Swapp.

Library of Congress Cataloging-in-Publication Data

Names: Frederick, Nicholas J., editor.
Title: His majesty and mission / edited by Nicholas J. Frederick and
    Keith J. Wilson.
Description: Provo : Religious Studies Center BYU, 2017.
Identifiers: LCCN 2016052350 | ISBN 9781944394127
Subjects: LCSH: Jesus Christ--Mormon interpretations. | Jesus Christ--
    Person and offices.
Classification: LCC BX8643.J4 H57 2017 | DDC 252/.09332--dc23 LC
    record available at https://lccn.loc.gov/2016052350

Contents

FOREWORD

Nicholas J. Frederick and Keith J. Wilson

While major world religions share many similar beliefs, Christianity sets itself apart from all others with the doctrine of the Resurrection. No other major religion asserts that a human being will receive a perfected body in the afterlife. In fact, some religious pundits opine that the doctrine of the Resurrection is the fulcrum upon which all of the Christian belief system rests—that Christianity rises or falls based on the reality of the Resurrection. Christian religious leaders of all walks have commented on the importance of the Resurrection, but perhaps none as forcefully as President Howard W. Hunter when he declared, "The doctrine of the Resurrection is the single most fundamental and crucial doctrine in the Christian religion. It cannot be overemphasized, nor can it be disregarded." Then in a warning tone he mentioned the consequences of disavowing or overlooking

Grant Romney Clawson, The Second Coming. © *Intellectual Reserve, Inc.*

the Resurrection. "Without the Resurrection, the gospel of Jesus Christ becomes a litany of wise sayings and unexplainable miracles."[1]

Charles Wesley, the great Methodist hymn writer, composed these inspired words expressing the majesty of the Resurrection:

> *Christ the Lord is risen today, Alleluia!*
> *Earth and heaven in chorus say, Alleluia!*
> *Raise your joys and triumphs high, Alleluia!*
> *Sing, ye heavens, and earth reply, Alleluia!*
> *Love's redeeming work is done, Alleluia!*
> *Fought the fight, the battle won, Alleluia!*
> *Death in vain forbids him rise, Alleluia!*
> *Christ has opened paradise, Alleluia![2]*

Accordingly, this volume and these Easter conferences are organized to enhance our celebration of the miracle of Easter. The essays published in this volume represent the papers presented at the annual Brigham Young University Easter Conferences in 2016 and 2017. In this volume, you will find the personal witnesses and testimonies of faithful disciples who have devoted their lives to understanding the majesty and mission of the Savior. May their careful, heartfelt, and inspired words take root in your heart and bring you to a deeper, more personal conviction of the central role Jesus Christ and his Resurrection have in the eternal welfare of all God's children.

Notes

1. Howard W. Hunter, "An Apostle's Witness of the Resurrection," *Ensign*, May 1986, 16–17.

2. Charles Wesley, "Christ the Lord Is Risen Today," *The United Methodist Hymnal*, no. 302.

THE LIVING CHRIST:

Apostolic Testimonies and Infinite Love

Elder Kevin J Worthen

Elder Kevin J Worthen is president of Brigham Young University and
an Area Seventy for The Church of Jesus Christ of Latter-day Saints.

Several years ago, I began to pay particular attention to the topical index at the front of the general conference issues of the *Ensign* magazine. It was part of an effort to determine the current focus of Church leaders. Upon receiving the magazine, I would turn to the topical index and note the two or three topics that were most frequently addressed. I would then determine how many of those talks were given by members of the First Presidency and Quorum of the Twelve. I would then add together the two numbers (the total number of talks on the topic, plus the number of those talks that were given by members of the First Presidency and Quorum of the Twelve), with the idea that the resulting total would give me a rough, general sense of the current focus and priorities of Church leaders, especially those fifteen brethren who have the sacred duty to act as prophets, seers, and revelators.[1]

In the twelve conferences from 2008 through 2013, there were a handful of topics that commanded the top spot, with the topics varying from conference to conference. During that time, the leading topics included "family," "adversity," "temples," "love," "Jesus Christ," "obedience," "faith," and "service." On average, the most discussed topic in a conference was addressed in just over seven talks, with just over five of those being given by members of the First Presidency and Quorum of the Twelve (i.e., the average of the highest total combined score was just under thirteen). The highest total combined score for a single topic in any conference was nineteen (twelve talks on the topic, with seven by members of the First Presidency and Quorum of the Twelve); the lowest combined total for a leading topic was nine.

Beginning with the May 2014 *Ensign* (containing the contents of the April 2014 general conference), there was a significant shift. In that April 2014 conference, one topic was addressed in fifteen talks, with ten of those by members of the Quorum of the Twelve and the First Presidency—a combined total of twenty-five, which nearly doubled the average of the leading topic in the previous twelve conferences. In the ensuing October 2014 conference, that same topic was addressed nineteen times, with eleven of those talks being given by prophets, seers, and revelators—a combined total of thirty. The trend has continued from there. In the April 2015 general conference, the same topic was addressed in seventeen talks, with eleven of those given by prophets, seers, and revelators (a combined total of twenty-eight). In October 2015, the combined total was twenty-eight (nineteen and nine); in April 2016 it was twenty-six (seventeen and nine); and in October 2016 it was an astounding thirty-seven (twenty-six and eleven). In each of these conferences, one topic drew much more attention than any leading topic in any single conference between 2008 and 2013, and in each conference the leading topic was the same. The topic? Jesus Christ.

This dramatic shift may well be the result of an editorial decision to use a more comprehensive and accurate method for categorizing the topics addressed in general conference— as my guess is that the Savior has been a major focus of general conference remarks for quite some time. But there can be little doubt that one of the major areas of focus for conference speakers in the past few years, especially members of the Quorum of the Twelve and First Presidency, has been the Lord Jesus Christ.

In one sense, that topic has been the main focus from the beginning of this dispensation. Jesus Christ is the core message of the restored gospel, the irreducible center of all we believe. As we read in section 76 of the Doctrine and Covenants, "And this is the gospel, the glad tidings, which the voice out of the heavens bore record unto us—that he came into the world, even Jesus, to be crucified for the world, and to bear the sins of the world, and to sanctify the world, and to cleanse it from all unrighteousness."[2] Or as Alma put it, "For behold, I say unto you there be many things to come; and behold, there is one thing which is of more importance than they all—for behold, the time is not far distant that the Redeemer liveth and cometh among his people."[3]

Further evidence that the message of Christ has been the central focus of prophets, seers, and revelators from the beginning of this dispensation to the present is found in the fact

that Elders D. Todd Christofferson[4] and M. Russell Ballard[5] included the following statement from Joseph Smith in their April and October 2014 conference addresses, respectively: "The fundamental principles of our religion are the testimony of the Apostles and Prophets, concerning Jesus Christ, that He died, was buried, and rose again on the third day, and ascended into heaven; and all other things which pertain to our religion are only appendages to it."[6]

It is instructive to note that Joseph Smith focused on the testimony of the apostles and prophets concerning Christ, rather than on just the facts concerning Christ and His mission.[7] There is special power and impact in the testimony prophets and apostles bear of Christ, for they are called to be "special witnesses of the name of Christ in all the world— thus differing from other officers in the church in the duties of their calling."[8] Thus, it is not surprising that this has been their focus at general conference and in all their ministry.

Understanding how central the responsibility of testifying of Christ is to the apostolic calling, we can more fully appreciate the blessing and significance of a remarkable revelatory document provided by those Apostles in our own generation. In 2000, all fifteen then-living modern-day Apostles issued a testimony of Christ as a group. I am not aware of any other time or manner in which such a collective testimony of the central core of the gospel has been given by those whose particular calling is to provide such a witness.

This declaration, titled "The Living Christ: The Testimony of the Apostles," was produced particularly for our time and circumstances. As Elder Robert D. Hales noted in 2013, "The world is moving away from the Lord faster and farther than ever before.

The adversary has been loosed upon the earth. We watch, hear, read, study, and share the words of prophets to be forewarned and protected. For example, 'The Family: A Proclamation to the World' was given long before we experienced the challenges now facing the family. 'The Living Christ: The Testimony of the Apostles' was prepared in advance of when we will need it most."[9]

Note the verb tenses Elder Hales used. The family proclamation was given before we experienced the challenges now facing (present tense) the family. "The Living Christ" was prepared in advance of when we will (future tense) need it the most. That prophetic pronouncement by Elder Hales, coupled with the enhanced emphasis on the Savior in recent conference addresses by the other prophets (including multiple references to Joseph Smith's characterization of the central role of such testimonies in the gospel message) invites us to become more familiar with the truths in that remarkable document.

The first sentence of "The Living Christ" sets forth in clear and simple terms the two basic features of that remarkable collective apostolic testimony. "As we commemorate the birth of Jesus Christ two millennia ago, we offer our testimony of [1] the reality of His matchless life and [2] the infinite virtue of His great atoning sacrifice."[10]

The rest of the document provides particular details about these two core features of Christ's central role in the plan of salvation. Each is worthy of extended consideration.

The Reality of His Matchless Life

Christ's life was truly matchless. That life "neither began in Bethlehem nor concluded on Calvary."[11] But I would like to focus on the importance of the reality of the matchless *mortal* period of His life, something that is becoming less accepted, even in Christianity.

Some Bible scholars now contest whether Jesus ever lived in mortality, propounding the view that Jesus was a fictional character.[12] Others, while conceding the fact that a being named Jesus did indeed live in the Holy Land, contend that His life wasn't matchless, arguing that He was not the kind of divine being the Gospel writers conveyed Him to be.[13] In the words of one commentator, these critics assert "that Jesus was a simple itinerant preacher who never claimed to be divine and whose 'resurrection' was in fact an invention of his disciples who experienced hallucinations of their master after his death."[14] Thus, while a generation or two ago it could be taken as a given among most of the American population that Jesus's mortal life was real and unparalleled, that may no longer be the case. For that reason, it is especially important that we have special witnesses who attest with divinely appointed power that He did actually live and that His life was as perfect as He claimed.

"The Living Christ" states forthrightly that Jesus actually "walked the roads of Palestine," that He actually "went about doing good."[15] He did that both to encourage us to "follow His example"[16] *and* to make it possible for Him to perform His great atoning sacrifice.

Talks on Easter talks normally, and correctly, focus on the two eternity-shaping events of the last week of the Savior's earthly sojourn that together constitute the core of His great Atonement—His suffering in Gethsemane and Golgotha and His subsequent Resurrection from the dead. Each of these two events is of supernal and everlasting importance to all beings who have ever lived on this world or on countless other worlds. Easter would not be Easter without those two events. Indeed, life would not be meaningful without them. Each is rightly the subject of volumes of inspired writings and teachings. But I think it important that we also focus part of our Easter worship on the preceding portions of His matchless mortal life because I believe they are also a part of His great atoning sacrifice. Christ did not come to earth only for the last week of His mortal journey. His life prior to that last week was not mere prelude. I believe those years of His life were also a central part of His atoning sacrifice in at least two senses.

First, Christ's entire earthly sojourn had to be lived in a way that qualified Him to perform the great atoning sacrifice. In order to be fully efficacious, His atoning sacrifice had to be perfect and complete, which required that Christ be free from any sin. But it also required that He achieve that sinless state in a mortal setting where temptations, disappointments, injustices, fatigue, and all other factors that have caused human beings to sin over the ages were fully experienced. As B. H. Roberts explained it, "The atonement must be made by deity, living man's life, enduring man's temptations, yet remaining without sin, that the sacrifice might be without spot or blemish."[17] He had to be "a man of sorrows, and acquainted with grief."[18] It was necessary that He be "in all points tempted like as we are, yet without sin."[19]

Thus, in one sense, every perfect choice, every perfect response, every perfect act in His completely perfect mortal life was part of His great atoning sacrifice. He not only gave His life in a manner that permitted Him to rescue all humankind from death and misery, He also lived His life in a way that made that infinite sacrifice possible. That reality of His matchless mortal life deserves some contemplation.

Second, during His mortal ministry, Christ provided an example of the things we need to do to make the power of His atoning sacrifice fully operative in our lives. The example began with His baptism, which, while not required to wash away His sins, nonetheless taught us the need to humble ourselves before the Father and to be obedient unto Him.[20] Thus, in the words of "The Living Christ," Christ "entreated all to follow His example,"[21] not just to show us what we could become, but also what we need to do to fully benefit from the atoning sacrifice that was to come.

Still, as important as His mortal life was in allowing us to take full advantage of His Atonement by following His example, there were some aspects of His mortal life that were truly "matchless" because only He could do them. Thus, the two features of "The Living Christ"—the reality of His matchless life and the infinite virtue of His great atoning sacrifice—overlap. He came to earth not just to provide an example of what we should do to inherit eternal life but also to make it possible for us to do so, despite our weaknesses and imperfections. Accordingly, at Easter, our attention inevitably shifts to the culminating events of Christ's life that form the core of his great atoning sacrifice.

The Infinite Virtue of His Great Atoning Sacrifice

Gratefully, we do not need to fully understand Christ's Atonement in order to benefit from it. I say *gratefully* because our finite minds cannot completely comprehend a sacrifice whose breadth and depth are infinite. As Elder Richard G.

Scott put it, "No mortal mind can adequately conceive, nor can human tongue appropriately express, the full significance of all that Jesus Christ has done for our Heavenly Father's children through His Atonement."[22]

Still, it is important and profitable for us to contemplate the monumental events of that sacrifice in an attempt to increase our limited comprehension, for such understanding can both better fit us to take full advantage of that infinite offering and provide us with the perspective and strength we need to endure the vicissitudes of life that inevitably occur. Elder Richard G. Scott also observed, "Your understanding of the Atonement and the insight it provides for your life will greatly enhance your productive use of all of the knowledge, experience, and skills you acquire in mortal life."[23] Furthermore, "our understanding of and faith in the Atonement of Jesus Christ will provide strength and capacity needed for a successful life. It will also bring confidence in times of trial and peace in moments of turmoil."[24]

With that in mind, let us consider two particular scenes from that portion of Christ's matchless mortal life that form the core of His great atoning sacrifice. The first occurred in the Garden of Gethsemane, where much of the Atonement was wrought. The scene was described by Elder Neal A. Maxwell:

> He said to His disciples, "Sit ye here, while I shall pray. And He taketh with him Peter and James and John, and began to be sore amazed and to be very heavy." (Mark 14:32, 33.) The Greek for "very heavy" is "depressed, dejected, in anguish." Just as the Psalmist had foreseen, the Savior was "full of heaviness." The heavy weight of the sins of all mankind were falling upon him.

He had been intellectually and otherwise prepared from ages past for this task. He is the Creator of this and other worlds. He knew the plan of salvation. He knew this is what it would come to. But when it happened, it was so much worse than even He had imagined![25]

It was in that setting that Christ offered perhaps the most powerful, most sublime, and most heartfelt prayers of all eternity. The scriptural record indicates that there were three distinct prayers.[26] We may not know the exact words that He used in those prayers, but there is an interesting progressive urgency and understanding portrayed in the differing wording found in each of the three Gospels that describe the scene.

Matthew records that Christ's original prayer began, "O my Father, *if it be possible, let this cup pass from me.*"[27] Christ was not anxious to go through the experience. It would not be surprising if He asked whether there was any other way that the plan could be effectuated. As Elder Maxwell observed, "Did Jesus hope there might be, as with Abraham, a ram in the thicket? We do not know, but the agony and the extremity were great."[28] The suffering was so great and burdensome that it would seem natural for Him to inquire whether there was some other means of accomplishing this most important work.

We next read in Mark a slightly different plea from the Savior: "Abba, Father, *all things are possible unto thee; take away this cup from me.*"[29] This plea seemed to remove the supposition implicit in the prayer from Matthew. Maybe it was not a question of possibility. As Jehovah, Christ had rhetorically, but instructively, asked Abraham, "Is anything too hard for the Lord?"[30] During His mortal ministry, Christ Himself had affirmatively asserted that "with God all things are possible."[31] The echoes of those teachings seem to be found in this particular prayer, which is more of an assertion (all things are possible) than a question (if it be possible). The use of the intimate "Abba," Daddy or Papa,[32] only heightens the confidence inherent in that assertion. "Daddy," He seems to say, "I know you can do all things, so please take this cup away from me."

But was it that simple? Was it possible for God to accomplish His work without exacting such a price from His Only Begotten Son? Could the full effects of the Atonement have been achieved by some other means? Perhaps the demands of the eternal law of justice could be satisfied in some other way. Maybe each individual could pay the price for his or her own sins, and the plan of salvation could be achieved without inflicting such cumulative pain on one who did not deserve it. Full answers to such ponderings are beyond our mortal reach, but there are several reasons to believe that there was no other way that the plan of salvation could be fully effectuated for God's children than by application of what Elder Maxwell called the "awful arithmetic of the Atonement."[33]

First, while it is clear that those who do not repent will pay the price for their own sins,[34] they will not be exalted[35] and will not reap the full benefits of Christ's atoning sacrifice. The power that Christ provides through His Atonement extends beyond the mere propitiation for our unrepented-of sins. It also enables us to be sanctified and changed. As Elder Dallin H. Oaks has noted, "Because of His atoning experience in mortality, our Savior is able to comfort, heal, and strengthen all men and women."[36] But such power comes about only through a sacrifice that is both eternal and infinite.[37] Christ could heal, comfort, and sanctify all of us only if He fully experienced and overcome everything that requires healing, comforting, and sanctification for every human being. And all of those must be overcome if God's purpose in exalting His children is to be realized. Thus, while each individual might be able to satisfy the demands of justice by paying for his or her individual sins, that alone would not achieve all that Christ made possible with His Atonement. Although, as a matter of pure power, God could have spared His Son the extreme agony he was undergoing, it likely would have been at the cost of the plan of salvation.[38]

Second, at a more abstract and yet more personal level, B. H. Roberts theorized that the extent of Christ's suffering and the scope of Heavenly Father's love for His Son were both so deep that there could not have possibly been a way for God to accomplish His work other than the infinite Atonement, which cost them both so much:

> The absolute necessity of the Atonement as it stands would further appear by the confidence one feels that if milder means could have been made to answer as an atonement, or if the satisfaction to justice could have been set aside, or if man's reconciliation with the divine order of things could have been brought about by an act of pure benevolence without other consideration, it undoubtedly would have been done; for it is inconceivable that either God's justice or his mercy would require or permit more suffering on the part of the Redeemer than was absolutely necessary to accomplish the end proposed. Any suffering beyond that which was absolutely necessary would be cruelty, pure and simple, and unthinkable in a God of perfect justice and mercy.[39]

Some may view the assertion that there was no other alternative for God but to sacrifice His Son to make His plan operative as inconsistent with the omnipotence of God. Yet, the mere fact that God operates in harmony with eternal laws does not mean He cannot accomplish everything He desires to do. It merely recognizes that He accomplishes those things through eternal laws, which He fully understands. Just as good lawyers can accomplish much through the use of laws even though they are not free to ignore them, a perfect "lawyer" can accomplish all things through the use of "perfect" laws. Indeed, only those who are "able to abide the *law of a celestial kingdom*" are able to "abide a celestial glory."[40]

In any event, the prayer recorded in Luke sets aside the perhaps unanswerable questions of possibilities raised in Matthew and Mark and comes to what was the critical point in the long run. "*Father, if thou be willing,*" Christ prayed, "*remove this cup from me.*"[41] In the end, it was not a matter of God's power or might, but of His will. And each of the three prayers made clear that Christ was ever willing to submit to that will. Echoing the sentiment He had expressed in the premortal council when the plan was described and accepted,[42] the Savior concluded each of His heartfelt pleas with the same, most important phrase: "Nevertheless, not my will, but thine, be done."[43] Whatever possible inferences might be drawn from the various words recorded in the different Gospels, each recorded prayer ended with the identical unwavering commitment by Christ that He would do whatever the Father willed Him to do.[44]

And it is clear that because of His great love for each of us, the Father's will was that Christ drink every last drop of the dregs of that bitter cup which the Atonement required.[45] But

He did not leave His Son to face that task alone. He sent an angel to comfort Christ in this moment of most agonizing distress.[46]

Contrast that tender moment in which the Father sent an angel to succor His Son through the incalculable agony of Gethsemane with the second scene a few hours later. After Christ had suffered through unjust trials, mocking, scourging and nailing to the cross, after He had entrusted His mother to John's tender care, forgiven those who nailed Him to the cross, and ministered to the thief at His side, he uttered perhaps the most heart-rending, poignant cry that ever ascended from this earth to the heavens above. As recorded in Mark, "And at the ninth hour Jesus cried with a loud voice, saying, Eloi, Eloi, lama sabachthani? which is, being interpreted, My God, my God, why hast thou forsaken me?"[47]

At that point, Abba—Daddy—was no longer there. For the first and likely only time in His mortal and probably premortal existence, the Son was completely cut off from His Father's presence. It was one thing to confront the reality that His Father wanted Him to go through the most taxing ordeal any being would ever face, but it was quite another to be abandoned by that Father in that trial.

As both Elder Holland and Elder Scott have asserted, it is possible that the Father was never closer to Christ than at this moment,[48] but He had to withdraw His influence entirely from His beloved Son. How difficult that must have been for the Father. As Elder Scott observed, "It is instructive to try to imagine what the Atonement required of both the Father and His willing Son" at such a time.[49]

As Elder Scott further observed, "we do not fully know"[50] all the reasons why this separation was required. However, let me suggest two reasons, both of which increase my appreciation for the Savior's great love for each of us. The first deals with the centrality of agency in the plan of salvation. Just as Heavenly Father needed to allow His disobedient and faithless children to make their own choices in the pre-earth life— even though that choice deprived them of their

Carl Bloch, Christ with Thorns.

ability to benefit from His plan of happiness—I believe Heavenly Father needed to allow His perfectly obedient, sinless Son to make His own choice about the Atonement. As Elder Robert D. Hales explained, "So that He could finally demonstrate that He was choosing for Himself, He was left alone. . . . At last, He exercised His agency to act, enduring to the end, until He could say, 'It is finished.'"[51]

Perhaps Christ had to be willing to carry out the atoning sacrifice not just because He knew His Father wanted Him to do so, but because He, the Savior, wanted to do so. Maybe it was not enough for Christ to know that God loved us enough that He wanted Christ to suffer incomprehensible pain to spare us the same. Maybe Christ had to decide for Himself that He loved us enough to do so, that He finished the Atonement not just because we were Heavenly Father's children whom God loved, but because we were Christ's brothers and sisters whom He loved. And thus He was left alone so there could be no doubt that it was not just Heavenly Father who so loved the world that He gave His only begotten Son,[52] but that Christ also so loved the world that He voluntarily gave His own life and being.

The second reason deals with the healing power of the Atonement. Christ suffered intensely so He would be able fully to comfort and heal us in our extremities. That sometimes overlooked effect of Christ's Atonement was prophesied by Alma. Describing the Savior's ministry, Alma declared, "And he shall go forth, suffering pains and afflictions and temptations of every kind; and this that the word might be fulfilled which saith he will take upon him the pains and the sicknesses of his people, . . . and he will take upon him their infirmities, that his bowels may be filled with mercy, according to the flesh, that he may know according to the flesh how to succor his people according to their infirmities." In some way that our finite minds cannot comprehend, Christ felt all the pains, the sufferings, the infirmities, the loneliness of every human being on this and countless other worlds. Why? So that he could "succor" His people.

The word *succor* is particularly apt. In Spanish it is *socorrer*—to give relief. The word also derives from the Latin *correre*, which means to run.[53] Thus, *to succor* can mean *to run to give relief*. I like to picture the Savior running to give us relief, anxious to share our burdens. And His being left without the Father's influence allows Him to do that, to say with perfect empathy, "I understand." He understands perfectly because He felt exactly what we feel in any situation. To paraphrase, without distorting, the teaching in the Doctrine and Covenants, "He descended below all things," and thus "he comprehended all things."[54]

As Elder Holland explained, "It was required, indeed it was central to the significance of the Atonement, that this perfect Son who had never spoken ill nor done wrong nor touched an unclean thing had to know how the rest of humankind—us, all of us—would feel when we did commit such sins. For His Atonement to be infinite and eternal, He had to feel what it was like to die not only physically but spiritually, to sense what it was like to have the divine Spirit withdraw, leaving one feeling totally, abjectly, hopelessly alone."[55] Regardless of the reasons, Christ was left alone. And when left on His own, He forged ahead and completed His mission, ending His mortal life by saying, "Father, it is finished, thy will is done."[56]

We do not know exactly what happened next, but our human experience provides some basis for positive conjecture. Elder Holland once described a scene at an airport where it was clear that a family was waiting the arrival of a returning missionary. He noted the presence of the usual participants, including the mother, younger brothers, girlfriend, and father, a man whom he described as "a man of the soil, with a suntan and large, work-scarred hands. His white shirt was a little frayed and was probably never worn except on Sunday." Elder Holland speculated to himself which of the group might be first to break ranks to greet the young returning elder. He thought it might be the mother, who had initially given the missionary life, or perhaps the girlfriend, who looked like she might need oxygen. But Elder Holland then explained:

It wasn't the mother, and it wasn't the girlfriend, and it wasn't the rowdy little brother. That big, slightly awkward,

quiet and bronzed giant of a man put an elbow into the rib-
cage of a flight attendant and ran, just simply ran, out onto
that apron and swept his son into his arms. . . .

[The missionary] was probably 6′2″ or so, but this big
bear of a father grabbed him, took him clear off his feet,
and held him for a long, long time. He just held him and
said nothing. The boy dropped his briefcase, put both arms
around his dad, and they just held each other very tightly.
It seemed like all eternity stood still, and for a precious
moment the Salt Lake City Airport was the center of the
entire universe. It was as if all the world had gone silent out
of respect for such a sacred moment.

And then I thought of God the Eternal Father watching
his boy go out to serve, to sacrifice when he didn't have to
do it, paying his own way, so to speak, costing everything
he had saved all his life to give. At that precious moment,
it was not too difficult to imagine that father speaking with
some emotion to those who could hear, "This is my Beloved
Son, in whom I am well pleased." And it was also possible
to imagine that triumphant returning son, saying, "It is finished. Father, into thy hands I commend my spirit."

Now, I don't know what kind of seven-league boots a
father uses to rush through the space of eternity. But even in
my limited imagination I can see that reunion in the heavens.[57]

But even that triumphal scene is not the end of the story. As
"The Living Christ" makes clear, "His life, which is central to
all human history, neither began in Bethlehem nor concluded
on Calvary." It is the living Christ of whom the Apostles testify. His Resurrection is the greatest single affirmation of His

Carl Bloch, Crucifixion.

divinity and the power and reach of His atoning sacrifice.[58] As President Howard W. Hunter once explained, "Without the Resurrection, the gospel of Jesus Christ becomes a litany of wise sayings and seemingly unexplainable miracles—but sayings and miracles with no ultimate triumph. No, the ultimate triumph is in the ultimate miracle: for the first time in the history of mankind, one who was dead raised himself into living immortality."[59]

Without the Resurrection, the plan would fail. And its reality is the greatest evidence that the plan is perfect. On one occasion, Elder Bruce R. McConkie asked the question, "How do you prove that Jesus is the Christ?" He then answered, "It all centers in the Resurrection." He then asked, "How do you prove the Resurrection?" His response: "It all centers in witnesses."[60]

Thus, it is not surprising that the apostolic testimony in "The Living Christ" attests that Christ "rose from the grave to 'become the firstfruits of them that slept' (1 Corinthians 15:20)." And as proof, they cite His appearances to earthly witnesses whose testimonies are recorded in scriptures, starting with "those He had loved in life" and those "He . . . ministered among . . . in ancient America" and extending to the modern day when "He and His Father appeared to the boy Joseph Smith, ushering in the long-promised 'dispensation of the fulness of time' (Ephesians 1:10)."

These, and other appearances, were designed not only to provide mortal witnesses to the reality that Christ had overcome death, but also to further His work "to bring to pass the immortality and eternal life of man,"[61] a work in which He is still personally involved. As "The Living Christ" states, "His priesthood and His Church have been restored to earth," with "'Jesus Christ himself being the chief corner stone' (Ephesians 2:20)."[62] That leadership role will continue into the future when "He will someday return to earth" to "rule as King of Kings and reign as Lord of Lords."[63]

Christ not only currently leads His Church, He is also active in our lives today—if we let Him. He knocks at the door and waits for us to invite Him into our lives,[64] and when we do, we will find the truth of the apostolic witness that

Harry Anderson, The Resurrection, © *Intellectual Reserve, Inc.*

"His way is the path that leads to happiness in this life and eternal life in the world to come."[65] May we join those same witnesses in heartfelt expression: "God be thanked for the matchless gift of His divine Son."[66]

Notes

1. I note that I then read all of the talks and attempted to form my own personal (hopefully inspired) impressions of which of the topics they addressed were most tailored to my weaknesses and challenges.

2. D&C 76:40–41.

3. Alma 7:7.

4. D. Todd Christofferson, "The Resurrection of Jesus Christ," *Ensign*, May 2014, 111–14.

5. M. Russell Ballard, "Stay in the Boat and Hold On!" *Ensign*, November 2014, 91.

6. *Teachings of Presidents of the Church: Joseph Smith* (Salt Lake City: The Church of Jesus Christ of Latter-day Saints, 2007), 49.

7. "Joseph Smith might have said that the fundamental principles of our religion are the *facts* or *evidence* concerning Jesus Christ. . . . But he did not choose those or other similar words. He said that the *testimonies* of the apostles and prophets concerning Jesus Christ provide the fundamental principles of our religion." Cecil O. Samuelson, "The Testimony of Jesus Christ," in *Celebrating Easter: The 2006 BYU Easter Conference*, ed. Thomas A. Wayment and Keith J. Wilson (Provo, UT: Religious Studies Center, 2006), 12.

8. D&C 107:23.

9. Robert D. Hales, "General Conference: Strengthening Faith and Testimony," *Ensign*, November 2013, 7.

10. "The Living Christ: The Testimony of the Apostles of the Church of Jesus Christ of Latter-day Saints," *Ensign*, March 2008, 43.

11. "The Living Christ," 43.

12. See Earl Doherty, *Jesus: Neither God nor Man—The Case for a Mythical Jesus* (Ottawa: Age of Reason Publications, 2009); Robert M. Price, *Deconstructing Jesus* (Amherst, NY: Prometheus Books, 1999); Robert M. Price, *Jesus Is Dead* (Austin, TX: American Atheist Press, 2012), 271–79.

13. See, e.g., Bart D. Ehrman, *How Jesus Became God: The Exaltation of a Jewish Preacher from Galilee* (New York: HarperOne, 2014), 2–3.

14. Robert Barron, "You're Wrong, Bart Ehrman," Real Clear Religion, 16 April 2014, http://www.realclearreligion.org/articles/2014/04/16/youre_wrong_bart_ehrman.html; Barron discusses Bart Ehrman's book *How Jesus Became God* in this article.

15. "The Living Christ," 43.

16. "The Living Christ," 43.

17. B. H. Roberts, *The Truth, The Way, The Life: An Elementary Treatise on Theology*, ed. John W. Welch (Provo, UT: BYU Studies, 1995), 432.

18. Isaiah 53:3; Mosiah 14:3.

19. Hebrews 4:15.

20. 2 Nephi 31:6. His example in this regard also made clear the indispensability of proper baptism for all who would be saved. "And now, if the Lamb of God, he being holy, should have need to be baptized by water, to fulfil all righteousness, O then, how much more need have we, being unholy, to be baptized, yea, even by water!" (2 Nephi 31:5).

21. "The Living Christ," 43.

22. Richard G. Scott, "He Lives! All Glory to His Name!," *Ensign*, May 2010, 76.

23. Scott, "He Lives! All Glory to His Name!," 76.

24. Scott, "He Lives! All Glory to His Name!," 77.

25. Neal A. Maxwell, "A Choice Seer," *Ensign*, August 1986, 14.

26. Matthew 26:44; Mark 14:41.

27. Matthew 26:39; emphasis added.

28. Maxwell, "A Choice Seer," 14.

29. Mark 14:36; emphasis added.

30. Genesis 18:14.

31. Matthew 19:26; see also Mark 10:27; Luke 18:27.

32. "In that most burdensome moment of all human history, with blood appearing at every pore and an anguished cry upon His lips, Christ sought Him whom He had always sought—His Father. 'Abba,' He cried, 'Papa,' or from the lips of a younger child, 'Daddy.' This is such a personal moment it almost seems a sacrilege to cite it. A Son in unrelieved pain, a Father His only true source of strength, both of them staying the course, making it through the night—together." Jeffrey R. Holland, "The Hands of the Fathers," *Ensign*, May 1999, 16.

33. Neal A. Maxwell, "Willing to Submit," *Ensign*, May 1985, 73.

34. See D&C 19:16–17, "I, God, have suffered these things for all, that they might not suffer if they would repent; but *if they would not repent they must suffer even as I*"; emphasis added.

35. Elder Bruce C. Hafen observed, "I once wondered if those who refuse to repent but who then satisfy the law of justice by paying for their own sins are then worthy to enter the celestial kingdom. The answer is no. The entrance requirements for celestial life are simply higher than merely satisfying the law of justice." Bruce C. Hafen, *The Broken Heart: Applying the Atonement to Life's Experiences* (Salt Lake City: Deseret Book, 2008), 7.

36. Dallin H. Oaks, "Strengthened by the Atonement of Jesus Christ," *Ensign*, November 2015, 64.

37. Alma 34:11–12.

38. God "had the power to remove the bitter cup from the Savior, but the consequences were unacceptable." Edwin W. Aldous, "A Reflection on the Atonement's Healing Power," *Ensign*, April 1987, 13.

39. Roberts, *The Truth, The Way, The Life*, 428.

40. D&C 88:22.

41. Luke 22:42; emphasis added.

42. Moses 4:2, "Father, thy will be done."

43. Luke 22:42.

44. Indeed, Christ came to earth for that purpose (see John 5:30; 3 Nephi 11:11, D&C 19:21).

45. D&C 19:16–19.

46. Luke 22:43. "Luke wrote that at a particular point, an angel appeared to strengthen Him. I do not know who that angel was, but what a great privilege to be at the side of the Son of God as He worked out the Atonement for the whole human family!" Maxwell, "A Choice Seer," 15.

47. Mark 15:34.

48. "With all the conviction of my soul I testify . . . that a perfect Father did *not* forsake His Son in that hour. Indeed, it is my personal belief that in all of Christ's mortal ministry the Father may never have been closer to His Son than in these agonizing final moments of suffering. Nevertheless, that the supreme sacrifice of His Son might be as complete as it was voluntary . . . the Father briefly withdrew from Jesus the comfort of His Spirit, the support of His personal presence." Jeffrey R. Holland, "And None Were with Him," *Ensign*, May 2009, 87–88. Elder Scott observed along the same lines: "I don't believe Father in Heaven forsook His Son on the cross. . . . The Father did not abandon His Son. He made it possible for His perfect Son to win the eternal fruits of the Atonement." Scott, "He Lives! All Glory to His Name!," 77.

49. Scott, "He Lives! All Glory to His Name!," 76.

50. Scott, "He Lives! All Glory to His Name!," 77.

51. Robert D. Hales, "Agency: Essential to the Plan of Life," *Ensign*, November 2010, 25.

52. John 3:16.

53. *Oxford English Dictionary Online*, "succour" v., etymology ("Latin *succurrĕre*, < suc- = sub-prefix 6 + currĕre to run;"); see also Jeffrey R. Holland, "'He Hath Filled the Hungry with Good Things,'" *Ensign*, November 1997, 64–66.

54. D&C 88:6.

55. Jeffrey R. Holland, "And None Were with Him," 88.

56. Joseph Smith Translation, Matthew 27:54.

57. Jeffrey R. Holland, "'I Stand All Amazed,'" *Ensign*, August 1986, 73; from an address given to Salt Lake Temple workers, 24 November 1985.

58. "The Resurrection of the Savior proves that He is the Son of God and that what He taught is real. 'He is risen, as he said.' There could be no stronger proof of His divinity than Him coming forth from the grave with an immortal body." Paul V. Johnson, "And There Shall Be No More Death," *Ensign*, May 2016, 122.

59. Howard W. Hunter, "An Apostle's Witness of the Resurrection," *Ensign*, May 1986, 16.

60. John H. Madsen, "Easter, the Lord's Day," in *With Healing in His Wings*, ed. Camille Fronk Olson and Thomas A. Wayment (Provo, UT: Religious Studies Center; Salt Lake City: Deseret Book, 2013), 40–41.

61. Moses 1:39.

62. "The Living Christ," 47.

63. "The Living Christ," 47.

64. Revelation 3:20.

65. "The Living Christ," 47.

66. "The Living Christ," 47.

STANDING
AS A WITNESS

Sheri Dew

Sheri Dew is executive vice president of Deseret Management Corporation
and CEO of Deseret Book Company.

Can anyone do justice to the majesty and mission, let alone
the Atonement, of Jesus Christ? Even the most spiritually gifted don't have the words or the understanding to fully
communicate who the Savior is and what He did for us. On
the other hand, the Holy Ghost can bear witness of Him with
such clarity and power that we can each know, without question, that Jesus Christ is our Savior. I pray that the Spirit will
whisper truth to all who desire to know more and feel more
about Him. The Spirit is always the teacher.

A couple of years ago, I was meeting with one of my
evangelical friends in Boston the week prior to the week of
Easter. As we concluded and pulled out our smartphones
to check calendars for a follow-up meeting, my friend said,

"Well, we can't talk next week, that's Holy Week. It will have to be after that." I then made the mistake of asking, "Do you not work at all next week?" When he looked at me as though I were an infidel, I quickly shifted and asked how he and his family observed Holy Week. They had a full slate of activities planned—some as a family and some at their church. I found myself wondering why we as a people—who look to the Savior as the center of everything we believe and do—don't seem to be as engaged in celebrating Easter as others are. I hope the reason is that we seek to worship the Lord and make Him the center of our lives every week of the year. But I was moved by my friend's devotion. What the Savior did for us in the Garden of Gethsemane, on Calvary, and in the Garden Tomb ought to mean that much, and more, to all of us.

The Prophet Joseph Smith put the significance of those events in perspective: "The fundamental principles of our religion are the testimony of the Apostles and Prophets, concerning Jesus Christ, that He died, was buried, and rose again the third day, and ascended into heaven; and all other things which pertain to our religion are only appendages to it."[1]

In his vision of the redemption of the dead, President Joseph F. Smith saw the delight of those on the other side of the veil who had departed "mortal life, firm in the hope of a glorious resurrection." He said, "I beheld that they were filled with joy and gladness, and were rejoicing together because the day of their deliverance was at hand. They were assembled awaiting the advent of the Son of God into the spirit world, to declare their redemption from the bands of death."[2] No wonder President Gordon B. Hinckley called what we celebrate at Easter the "greatest victory of all time, the victory

Harry Anderson, Christ in Gethsemane. © *Intellectual Reserve, Inc.*

over death. . . . Towering above all mankind stands Jesus the Christ, the King of glory."[3]

With those words as a foundation—that "towering above *all mankind* stands Jesus the Christ"—may I share two recent experiences? Last year during the Christmas holidays, I attended an event where Elder Quentin L. Cook spoke. The audience that night was filled with men and women who

have devoted their lives to the Lord. It would be impossible
to calculate the breadth and depth of service that particular
group has rendered as General Authorities, general officers,
and priesthood and auxiliary leaders on every level of Church
government. On the face of it, you wouldn't think that audience needed motivation to testify of truth. And yet that night
Elder Cook told us that we needed to do two things much
better: first, defend the Prophet Joseph Smith; and second,
bear witness that Jesus is the Christ.

Elder Cook didn't stop there. He brought with him a
white-gloved archivist from the Church History Library
who displayed two intriguing artifacts: a page of the original
manuscript of the Book of Mormon and a journal written
in Joseph's hand. I had seen pages from the original Book of
Mormon manuscript before, but this time something struck
me—probably because the manuscript page was displayed
side by side with the journal, which was open to an entry
Joseph had made. The journal page had changes—words
crossed out, insertions, and so on—but there was not one
word changed on that long page of Book of Mormon manuscript. Not one.

That caught my attention. I've been in the publishing
business for almost forty years and have worked with many
of the most spiritually gifted communicators in our culture:
talented and inspired leaders, thinkers, speakers, and writers. I have sat across the desk from all of them and reviewed
literally thousands of their manuscripts. But in all these years,
one thing I have never seen is a manuscript with no changes.
I have had authors tell me their words are perfect, but they
never are. It is much more typical for even the most gifted

writers to write and rewrite ad nauseam. And yet, on that December evening, I was looking at an unchanged manuscript page recorded by scribes as Joseph translated the book by inspiration.[4]

For me, it was a piece of evidence supporting the Prophet's account of the coming forth of the Book of Mormon. Even still, my witness of that sacred book is not based on seeing manuscript pages. A spiritual witness is never based on tangible evidence. A witness of truth comes as the Holy Ghost speaks to our minds and to our hearts.[5] Revelation necessarily includes both, because intellect alone cannot produce a testimony. You cannot convince yourself of something your heart does not feel. It is only when the Spirit bears witness to our hearts and minds in the way only the Holy Ghost can that we can know for sure that something is true.

Turning now to my second experience, I have a dear and devout friend, not of our faith, whom I met years ago when we served together as delegates to a commission at the United Nations. In that foreign environment, she took me under her wing, and we have been friends ever since. My friend recently had an assignment that brought her in and out of Utah for several months. I didn't realize it, but she was in Salt Lake City the weekend of the general women's meeting last spring. A friend offered her a ticket to the meeting, and she went alone. Not long afterwards, we had lunch together, and she told me she had attended our meeting and was still thinking about it. I asked what had lingered with her, and she said, "Well, there are four things. Let me list them in ascending order of importance.

"First, everyone was *so* friendly. I felt very welcome. Second, I was surprised to find every woman in Sunday dress. I never see that at church these days. Third, I loved that everyone who spoke quoted scripture. I wish more of that happened in my church." Then she paused and said, "Most of all, I was taken with the fact that everyone said that they 'witnessed,' or something like that. What was it they said?" I responded that each speaker had borne witness that Jesus is the Christ and that His gospel has been restored. She paused again, as if trying to take it all in, and then said, "I have never heard anything quite like that before. That moved me."

I have not been able to stop thinking about the intersection of these two experiences: Elder Cook's charge to bear witness of Christ, and my friend's reaction to hearing faithful men and women do so. Consider the miracle of it! As men and women who have received the gift of the Holy Ghost,[6] we can know things. In a world filled with loud and articulate but often misinformed voices, we can discern what is true and what is not.

At times, when one of life's blows has left me reeling spiritually, I have said to myself, "Sheri, what do you know for sure?" And then I list those things: "I know that God is my Father, that Jesus is the Christ and that His Church has been restored. I know that Joseph Smith was a prophet, that the Book of Mormon is the word of God, and that priesthood power is real. I know the living prophet is a prophet." Some days, I can't go much further than that. But because the Spirit has borne witness to me of those truths again and again, I know they are true. So I have a foundation to fall back on and to build from.

Jon McNaughton, The Savior. © *Intellectual Reserve, Inc.*

We can bear witness only of what we know. We cannot testify of a wish or a hope or even a belief. We can express a hope, a wish, or a belief. But in order to bear witness of something such that the Holy Ghost ratifies our words, we must know what is true by the confirmation of the Spirit to our minds and hearts. Thus, we cannot stand as witnesses of Jesus Christ unless we can bear witness of Him. And we can bear witness only if we receive a witness from the Spirit that the Savior indeed "rose again the third day"[7] and that Jesus Christ is exactly who the prophets and apostles say He is. We can defend the faith only if we have faith.

This, then, begs two questions: How do we gain an unyielding spiritual witness that Jesus is the Christ? And what happens to us when we understand what He did for us?

First, how do we gain a witness that Jesus is the Christ? According to Elder Bruce R. McConkie, "The Atonement of Christ is the most basic and fundamental doctrine of the gospel, and it is the least understood of all our revealed truths. Many of us have a superficial knowledge and rely upon the Lord and His goodness to see us through the trials and perils of life. But if we are to have faith like that of Enoch and Elijah, we must believe what they believed, know what they knew, and live as they lived."[8]

How can we know what Elijah and Enoch knew about Christ? I believe the answer to that question lies in another question: Are you willing to engage in a wrestle? In an ongoing spiritual wrestle? The requirement to wrestle spiritually is not unique to our day. Enos described the "wrestle which [he] had before God, before [he] received a remission of [his] sins."[9] Alma described "wrestling with God in mighty prayer, that he would pour out his Spirit upon the people" of Ammonihah.[10]

Look at the life of any prophet, and you'll find lots of spiritual wrestling. Imagine the pleadings of Joseph, who was sold into Egypt by jealous brothers; or Noah, as he and his family boarded an ark with only partial knowledge of what lay ahead. Can you picture Brigham Young's supplications as he led a band of beleaguered converts on a trek through uncharted territory to a place he'd only seen in vision? The Lord can open the "eyes of our understandings."[11] He can reveal "all mysteries" and the "wonders of eternity."[12] But He isn't likely to do any of those things unless we ask, seek, and ponder. He will not force us to progress.

President Spencer W. Kimball taught that "man cannot discover God or his ways by mere mental processes. . . . Why, oh, why do people think they can fathom the most complex spiritual depths without the necessary experimental and laboratory work accompanied by compliance with the laws that govern it? Absurd it is, but you will frequently find popular personalities, who seem never to have lived a single law of God, discoursing . . . [about] religion. How ridiculous for such persons to attempt to outline for the world a way of life! . . . One cannot know God nor understand his works or plans unless he follows the laws which govern."[13]

One of the governing rules of spiritual inquiry is that the Lord expects us to "exercise [our] agency," as Elder Richard G. Scott taught, to "authorize the Spirit to teach [us]."[14] The scriptures repeatedly urge us to "ask, and it shall be given you; seek, and ye shall find; knock, and it shall be opened unto you."[15] One of the best ways to engage in a spiritual wrestle is to ask enlightened questions. Sometimes we act as though we're afraid of probing questions about our beliefs, our doctrine, and our practices. But surely the first lesson of the Restoration is that the Father and the Son respond to sincere questions, asked in faith. Questions are good. Questions are good if they are enlightened questions, asked in a spirit of faith, and asked of credible spiritual sources. That is why it is crucial to "search diligently in the light of Christ that [we] may know good from evil."[16]

Joseph Smith spoke about seeking truth from the purest of sources: "I have an old edition of the New Testament in the Hebrew, Latin, German, and Greek languages. . . . I thank God I have got this old book, but I thank him more for the gift of the Holy Ghost. . . . The Holy Ghost . . . comprehends more than all the world; and I will associate myself with Him."[17] The Apostle Paul taught the same thing: "Ye may all prophesy. . . . Covet to prophesy."[18] Every seeking member of the Church can and should be receiving revelation for his or her own life.

Questions are good because they lead to answers, to knowledge, and to revelation.[19] Said President Henry B. Eyring: "We all know that human judgment and logical thinking will not be enough to get *answers to the questions* that matter most in life. We need revelation from God. . . . We need not just one flash of light and comfort, but we need the continuing blessing of communication with God."[20] In this regard, President Boyd K. Packer often said that "if all you know is what you see with your natural eyes and hear with your natural ears, then you will not know very much."[21]

Not asking questions of God is far more dangerous than asking them. The scriptures are filled with warnings like this one: "Wo be unto him that saith: We have received, and we need no more."[22] A pattern of not seeking help from heaven blocks revelation and leaves a person alone with downward spiraling thoughts or seeking out like-minded doubters in the blogosphere. And that always retards spiritual growth and stymies faith. Alma taught that many may know the mysteries of God but that those who harden their hearts receive less and less until they "know nothing concerning his mysteries; and then they are taken captive by the devil, and led by his will down to destruction. Now this is what is meant by the chains of hell."[23] In other words, spiritual death begins with knowing nothing. Or, said another way, sin makes you stupid—and so does the rejection of truth. Truman Madsen wrote of scholar B. H. Roberts that "he could find nothing in the scriptures . . . to excuse anyone from brain sweat and from the *arduous lifetime burden* of seeking 'revelation upon revelation, knowledge upon knowledge.'"[24]

When we are willing to wrestle with questions—and especially when we are wrestling to understand truth—we can count on learning things. And often what we learn is how the Lord has been working in our lives all along. Two years ago, I was invited to deliver the keynote address at the BYU Women's Conference on the subject of grace, and I was terrified. I knew I did not understand grace well enough to teach it in a way that the Spirit could endorse the message. So I went to work. I fasted and prayed, pored over the scriptures, went to the temple, and pleaded for spiritual enlightenment. I was essentially asking for the grace, or power, of the Lord to help me understand the grace of the Lord. It was a grueling process, particularly as the conference neared and I had volumes of notes but no talk. But then, little by little, the Spirit not only clarified points of doctrine but brought to my mind experiences I'd had that were clearly manifestations of grace—though I had not realized it at the time. In the grace of the Lord, I saw more clearly than I ever had how frequently He had been lifting and healing me. When we are willing to wrestle spiritually, we're in a better position to help others—but we are always the ones who benefit most.

In addition to knowledge and revelation, a spiritual wrestle also leads to greater faith. There are those who insist that faith is nothing more than a spiritual crutch. But faith is what ignites all spiritual growth. Although the Lord will reveal many things to us, He has never told His covenant people everything about everything. We are admonished to "doubt not, but be believing."[25] But "doubting not" does not mean understanding everything.

Consider the verse that sent Joseph to the grove—"If any of you lack wisdom, let him ask of God, that giveth to all men liberally, and upbraideth not; and it shall be given him." James then added this stipulation: "But let him ask in faith, nothing wavering."[26] Doubting is not synonymous with the pursuit of truth nor is it synonymous with having questions. Doubt is the rejection of faith. As covenant sons and daughters—as people of faith—we are required to have faith, to live by faith, and to "overcome by faith."[27] Learning by faith is every bit as crucial as learning by study, because there are some things we cannot learn from a book. There are some truths we can understand in full only when we exercise and experience faith.[28]

A woman kneeling in prayer. © *Intellectual Reserve, Inc.*

Therefore, once the Spirit has borne witness to you of truth—any truth—and particularly that Jesus is the Christ, that His gospel has been restored, that Joseph Smith was a prophet, and that the Book of Mormon is scripture, then you know the gospel is true because the Spirit has borne witness of the foundational truths that comprise a testimony. Other questions that arise—whether they are doctrinal, proce-dural, or personal—are not about whether or not you have a testimony. They are about personal, spiritual growth. That is why questions asked in faith are never a threat to testimony.

They are opportunities to strengthen testimony. It is also why doubting promptings of the Spirit creates an entirely new set of problems.

There is a tendency to assume that questions about doctrine or Church procedures or unfulfilled personal blessings are somehow connected to our testimonies. And it can sometimes feel that way. If you have been pleading for healing or marriage or a child without a fulfillment of those pleadings, it can be tempting to wonder if God is real, if He's listening, or if He cares. Those wonderings, left in isolation, can threaten testimony. But once you have received a spiritual witness of the truths that form the foundation of testimony, when questions arise—even the thorniest questions about our doctrine or history or positions on sensitive issues, or the aching pleadings of our lives—those questions are about personal growth. They are not red flags suggesting that the gospel isn't true after all. They are opportunities to receive revelation and increase faith. Questions, especially the tough ones, can propel us to engage in a spiritual wrestle that deepens our witness that Jesus is the Christ. Without wrestling and plain old hard work, even God can't make us grow—or at least, He won't.[29]

So how do we gain an unyielding witness that Jesus is the Christ? Through an ongoing spiritual wrestle. My life has been filled with spiritual wrestling—not because of any great valor on my part but because I have yearned to understand why certain things were happening to me, and why others were not. I have fasted and prayed, spent countless hours in the temple, and pored over the scriptures to find peace. My efforts have not magically produced all of the blessings I desire. But I have learned for myself that Jesus Christ is not only *the* Savior but *my* Savior.

Which leads to the second question: What happens to us when we understand what the Savior did for us? I recently met a young mother in the middle of a painful divorce who told me that, as difficult as it was, she was growing spiritually in a way she'd never experienced. "I had always known that if I repented, the Lord would forgive me," she said. "But I did not realize that the Atonement could heal me of my sadness and mistakes. This is the first time I've realized that He has power to heal my heart."

I was in my early thirties when I experienced a crushing heartache. An opportunity to marry evaporated overnight, and I was devastated, adrift in a sea of hurt and loneliness. I didn't handle myself very well during that painful season. I flailed about emotionally and wallowed in anger, including at the Lord, for "letting me down." In the midst of that ordeal, however, I received a priesthood blessing in which I was told that this trial was "a gift." "You've got to be kidding," I thought. "A gift?" I wrestled for understanding and for peace. Neither came quickly, but during the process, I began to understand for the first time that, as Elder Bruce C. Hafen taught, the Atonement was not just for sinners.[30] Because the Lord took upon Himself our sins, weaknesses, mistakes, and agonies, there is godly power available to help His followers deal with all kinds of pain.

That "gift" thirty years ago altered the trajectory of my life. For the first time, I understood what Malachi and Nephi meant when they prophesied that the Savior would rise "with healing in his wings."[31] I truly appreciated Isaiah's prophecy that He would give those who mourn in Zion "beauty for ashes" and the "oil of joy for mourning."[32] I knew that the Savior came to "heal the brokenhearted,"[33] that He took upon Himself my pain and would "succor," or run to, me.[34]

Since that time, I have thought of the Atonement in large measure as a doctrine of healing. The Savior will heal us from sin, *if* we repent. He will heal us from weakness, sadness, and loneliness; from hurt, fear, and mistakes; from the emotional and spiritual bruises of attempting to live covenant lives in a spiritually hostile world; from the effects of unfairness, abuse, and the sins of others; from disappointment, a lack of courage, or wavering faith. As President Howard W. Hunter declared, "Whatever Jesus lays his hands upon lives. If Jesus lays his hands upon a marriage, it lives. If he is allowed to lay his hands upon the family, it lives."[35]

Knowing that we would need and long for healing, the Savior extended this soothing invitation: "Will ye not now return unto me, . . . and be converted, that I may heal you? . . . Behold, mine arm of mercy is extended towards you, and whosoever will come, him will I receive."[36] The most sure way to gain access to the Savior's healing, strengthening power is to make covenants with Him and then keep them. When Alma's people were being held captive, the Lord "came to them in their afflictions, saying: Lift up your heads and be of good comfort, for I know of the covenant which ye have made unto me; and I will covenant with my people and deliver them out of bondage." He then promised to ease their burdens such that they could not feel them. "And this will I do," the Lord explained, "that ye may stand as witnesses for me hereafter, and that ye may know of a surety that I, the Lord God, do visit my people in their afflictions."[37]

John Scott, Jesus Christ Visits the Americas. © *Intellectual Reserve, Inc.*

The most powerful way to gain a witness of the healing power of Jesus Christ is to experience His healing power. And often that comes as we engage in a spiritual wrestle.

While I was serving in the Relief Society general presidency, we had the opportunity to attend sessions of General Authority training held in conjunction with general conference. I never took that glorious privilege for granted. But there was one training session that affected me in a very personal way. The topic for that session was strengthening families, and it was conducted by a General Authority who invited a great deal of audience participation.

From the outset, whenever someone responded to a question and used the word *woman* to describe a female's role in the family, the conducting officer would tell that person to use the word *mother* instead. The same was true with reference to men, whom he wanted referred to as fathers. At first

I didn't think much of it, but as the morning wore on and the point was repeatedly made that women were mothers and men were fathers, I began to shrink in my chair. I doubt anyone else even thought about it, but I was painfully aware of the fact that I was the only person in the room who was neither a mother nor a father.

By the time the meeting ended, I could not get out of that room fast enough. I hurried back to my office, closed the door, and wept. I had served as a ward and stake Relief Society president and as a member of the Relief Society general board. I had never felt that I didn't belong in the Church—until that morning. And, to make it worse, I felt excluded by prophets, seers, and revelators, which in that moment made me wonder how the Lord felt about me. Unfortunately, I began to stew about the meeting. At first, I was just hurt, but the hurt festered into anger. I could not understand how "the Brethren" could disenfranchise so many members. There was no one I could talk to about how I felt. I couldn't quite picture telling my bishop that I was upset with a General Authority. So I just stewed.

This went on for months, until I began working on the address I was to give at the upcoming general Relief Society meeting. I prayed, pondered, fasted, and went to the temple for weeks and—nothing. No inspiration. No ideas. Nothing. As the days raced by, I began to panic. Finally, I had one clear impression that was also a reprimand: I needed to resolve my feelings about that General Authority. I knew it was true, and in a spirit of humility I got on my knees and asked the Lord to forgive me for the resentment I'd been nurturing. And then I asked the Lord the question I should have asked months before: Did I miss something in that meeting?

Two days later I had another clear impression—
that I should speak in the general Relief Society meeting
about, of all things, motherhood. "Seriously?" I thought.
But the impression was clear, so I went to work. I searched
the scriptures and went to the temple again and again. In
other words, I wrestled. I wrestled to understand the doctrine of motherhood, and I wrestled with my own feelings
about that doctrine.

And guess what I learned? That General Authority had
been right. That every woman, regardless of her life circumstances, has been divinely endowed with the gift and
the gifts of motherhood. Eve was named the Mother of All
Living before she ever bore a child on this earth.[38] Motherhood is the essence of who women are. It defines our
identity, our divine stature, and the unique traits our Father
gave us. This led to an address titled "Are We Not All Mothers?"[39] For the first time in my life, I not only understood
the doctrine of motherhood but experienced healing about
not bearing children in this life. I am not saying that the
longing for a family went away, because it did not. But
the deep pain I had tried to suppress for years was gone. In
response to my repentance and wrestling, the Savior healed
that pain while teaching me the truth about the eternal
nature of women.

Moroni commended us to "seek this Jesus of whom the
prophets and apostles have written."[40] What is different for
you and me when we understand what the Savior did for us?
The answer is, everything.

Everything changed because of Jesus Christ. Everything
is better because of Him. Everything about our Father's plan

became operable because of Him. Everything about life is manageable, especially the painful parts, because of Him. Everything is possible because of Him. Every heavenly power and privilege is available to us because of Him and His gospel. The Savior changed everything for all who are willing to make covenants with Him and then keep them.

Without the Savior and His gospel, we would have no hope—no access to any kind of heavenly power. No family that extends beyond the grave and therefore no hope of anything but the emotionally crippling state of eternal singleness. We would have no escape from sin, from our mistakes, or from the binding cords of the devil. And all of this means that we would have no peace. No joy. No happiness. No healing. No resurrection. No possibility of having our spirits and bodies reunited forever. No reunion of the faithful. No possibility of eternal life. No future.

Brigham Young said that prior to the Restoration of the gospel the whole of Christian doctrine could be "simmered down . . . into a snuff box. . . . But when I found Mormonism, I found it was higher than I could reach . . . deeper than I was capable of comprehending, and calculated to expand the mind, and lead mankind from truth to truth, from light to light, from grace to grace, and exalt him . . . to become associated with Gods and the angels."[41]

I know that this is true. I have pleaded with the Lord so many times, for so many years, for help and understanding. He has walked with me and stayed with me when I felt no hope. He has sent His angels to be with me. He has healed my heart again and again and is responsible for every moment of joy.

None of this would be possible absent what happened in Gethsemane, on Calvary, and in the tomb.

He is risen! He is risen!
Tell it out with joyful voice.
He has burst his three days' prison;
Let the whole wide earth rejoice.
Death is conquered; man is free.
Christ has won the victory.[42]

Of that victory, I bear my witness. I can stand as a witness of Him because I have received a witness—again and again—that Jesus Christ is real and that His Atonement was perfect and infinite. I have experienced His healing power again and again.

I testify that the Savior is going to come again and that all who can stand as witnesses of Him have the profound privilege of helping prepare the earth for His return.

May we engage in the wrestle to gain an unflinching witness of Jesus Christ. May we gain a witness so that we can stand as witnesses of Him "at all times and in all things and in all places."[43] May we defend the faith because we have experienced the power of having faith in the Savior of the world.

Notes

1. *Teachings of Presidents of the Church: Joseph Smith* (Salt Lake City: The Church of Jesus Christ of Latter-day Saints, 2007), 49. Joseph Smith's statement continued: "But in connection with these, we believe in the

gift of the Holy Ghost, the power of faith, the enjoyment of the Spiritual gifts according to the will of God, the restoration of the house of Israel, and the final triumph of truth."

2. D&C 138:14–16.

3. Gordon B. Hinckley, "This Glorious Easter Morn," *Ensign*, May 1996, 67. President Hinckley also declared that "there would be no Christmas if there had not been Easter. The babe Jesus of Bethlehem would be but another baby without the redeeming Christ of Gethsemane and Calvary, and the triumphant fact of the Resurrection" ("The Wondrous and True Story of Christmas," *Ensign*, December 2000, 5). President Howard W. Hunter added that "without the Resurrection, the Gospel of Jesus Christ becomes a litany of wise sayings and seemingly unexplainable miracles" ("An Apostle's Witness of the Resurrection," *Ensign*, May 1986, 15). Indeed, as Joseph Smith saw in vision, the Savior "came into the world . . . to be crucified for the world, and to bear the sins of the world, and to sanctify the world, and to cleanse it from all unrighteousness" (D&C 76:41).

4. Speaking as a publisher, I do not believe that any man could have authored page after page of unaltered manuscript in less than ninety days to bring forth the Book of Mormon.

5. See D&C 8:2–3.

6. See 1 Nephi 13:37.

7. *Teachings of Presidents of the Church: Joseph Smith*, 49.

8. Bruce R. McConkie, *A New Witness for the Articles of Faith* (Salt Lake City: Deseret Book, 1985), xv; emphasis added.

9. Enos 1:2.

10. Alma 8:10. Paul told the Ephesians that "we wrestle not against flesh and blood, but against principalities, against powers, against the rulers of the darkness of this world, against spiritual wickedness in high places" (Ephesians 6:12).

11. D&C 76:19.

12. See D&C 76:7–8.

13. Spencer W. Kimball, "Absolute Truth" (BYU devotional address, 6 September 1977, found at www.speeches.byu.edu).

14. Richard G. Scott, *21 Principles: Divine Truths to Help You Live by the Spirit* (Salt Lake City: Deseret Book, 2013), 95–96.

15. See Matthew 7:7; 3 Nephi 14:7; 3 Nephi 27:29.

16. Moroni 7:19.

17. Joseph Smith, history, 1838–1856, vol. E-1, Church History Library, Salt Lake City, 1972–73. Joseph Smith also said, in a frequently quoted, important statement: "God hath not revealed anything to Joseph, but what he will make known unto the Twelve, and even the least Saint may know all things as fast he is able to bear them, for the day must come when no man need say to his neighbor know ye the Lord for all shall know him, . . . from the least to the greatest" (Joseph Smith, history, 1838–1856, vol. C-1, Church History Library, 8; see also *Teachings of Presidents of the Church: Joseph Smith*, 268).

18. 1 Corinthians 14:31, 39.

19. Questions are good because they lead to light and truth, and "light and truth forsake that evil one" (D&C 93:37).

20. Henry B. Eyring, "Continuing Revelation," *Ensign*, November 2014, 70.

21. As quoted by David A. Bednar, "Quick to Observe," in *Brigham Young University 2005–2006 Speeches* (Provo, UT: Brigham Young University, 2006), 24.

22. 2 Nephi 28:27. The Lord also said, as a further example of this point, "Wo unto the deaf that will not hear; for they shall perish. Wo unto the blind that will not see; for they shall perish also" (2 Nephi 9:31–32).

23. Alma 12:10–11. Alma also made it clear that those who do not harden their hearts will receive more and more until they know the mysteries of God "in full."

24. Truman G. Madsen, *Defender of the Faith: The B. H. Roberts Story* (Salt Lake City: Bookcraft, 1980), 387; emphasis added.

25. Mormon 9:27.

26. James 1:5–6.

27. D&C 76:53.

28. See D&C 88:118. Faith does not stand still. It is either increasing or disappearing. As President Henry B. Eyring has said, "Faith has a short shelf life" ("Spiritual Preparedness: Start Early and Be Steady," *Ensign*, November 2005, 39).

29. President Howard W. Hunter explained that "the development of spiritual capacity does not come with the conferral of authority. There must be desire, effort, and personal preparation. This requires, of course, . . . fasting, prayer, searching the scriptures, experience, meditation, and a hungering and thirsting after the righteous life." *Teachings of Presidents of the Church: Howard W. Hunter* (Salt Lake City: The Church of Jesus Christ of Latter-day Saints, 2015), 82.

30. See Bruce C. Hafen, *The Broken Heart: Applying the Atonement to Life's Experiences* (Salt Lake City: Deseret Book, 2008).

31. 2 Nephi 25:13.

32. Isaiah 61:3.

33. See Luke 4:18 and Jacob 2:8 about healing the "wounded soul."

34. Alma 7:11–12.

35. Howard W. Hunter, "Reading the Scriptures," *Ensign*, November 1979, 65.

36. 3 Nephi 9:13–14.

37. Mosiah 24:13–14.

38. Moses 4:26.

39. See Sheri L. Dew, "Are We Not All Mothers?," *Ensign*, November 2001, 96–98.

40. See Ether 12:41.

41. Leonard J. Arrington, *Brigham Young: American Moses* (Urbana: University of Illinois Press, 1986), 78n72.

42. Cecil Frances Alexander, "He Is Risen!" *Hymns* (Salt Lake City: The Church of Jesus Christ of Latter-day Saints, 1985), no. 199.

43. Mosiah 18:9.

PREACHING JESUS, AND HIM CRUCIFIED

Eric D. Huntsman

Eric D. Huntsman is a professor of ancient scripture at
Brigham Young University and the coordinator of the
Ancient Near Eastern Studies Program.

On Good Friday we gather to commemorate all that Jesus Christ did for us in the final week of his life, and we prepare to celebrate his Resurrection on Easter morning. From third to eleventh grade, I grew up in the greater Pittsburgh area, where most of my friends were Roman Catholics or mainline Protestants. This was an area where we always had fish on Fridays in the school cafeteria and where many of my friends were excused from school on Good Friday. Growing up as a member of the LDS diaspora, I used to wonder, "What is so good about Good Friday?" I knew that it was the day when we commemorated that Jesus had died for us on the cross, but celebrating it as a holiday was not part of either my church or family traditions.

Francisco de Zurbarán, Crucifixion.

56

Now it is, and I would ask the question "Why *not* Good Friday?" Only over time have I come to understand better the meaning of this day. Only as an adult did I come to learn that "good" here might have been an archaic way of referencing God, as when we say "good-bye," which originally meant "God be with ye" or "Go with God." That aside, it is good because it was "holy" Friday, the day when, as Paul says in Romans 5:8–12, we were reconciled to God by the death of his Son. The Crucifixion, which stands starkly and painfully as the central feature of this day, figures as one of the central features of the teaching of Paul, who wrote, "For I determined not to know any thing among you, save Jesus Christ, and him crucified" (1 Corinthians 2:2) and "God forbid that I should glory, save in the cross of our Lord Jesus Christ, by whom the world is crucified unto me, and I unto the world" (Galatians 6:14).

A number of factors have probably contributed to why Latter-day Saints do not formally celebrate Good Friday as a holiday per se. Generally, as a faith community we tend to avoid emphasizing or focusing on all the suffering connected with the last day of Jesus' mortal life. Many of the earliest Latter-day Saints were descended from New England Puritans, who largely avoided marking holy days, some of them even avoiding celebrating Christmas. Perhaps most significantly, culturally our faith community has not featured the cross in its iconography. Nevertheless, Book of Mormon features prophecies about Jesus's rejection, abuse, false judgment, and Crucifixion such as 1 Nephi 19:9, 2 Nephi 6:9, and Mosiah 3:9.

In regard to the cross, Gaye Strathearn, associate professor of ancient scripture, and Robert L. Millet, professor emeritus of ancient scripture and former dean of Religious Education, have done important work examining many of the historical, theological, and cultural issues involved in our understanding of the use of the means of our Lord's death as a symbol for his atoning work. After reviewing historical aspects of crucifixion as a form of execution and how New Testament authors employ its imagery in her 2013 *Religious Educator* article "The Crucifixion: Reclamation of the Cross," Strathearn reflects on reasons why the cross should be meaningful to Latter-day Saints. These include the fact that the events on the cross were integral parts of the Atonement, that Christ's being lifted up upon it was a symbol of God's love for us, that the invitation to "take up our cross" was a symbol of discipleship, and that the signs of the Crucifixion were so significant that he retained them in his resurrected body.[1]

In his essay "What Happened to the Cross?" in a 2007 Deseret Book volume of the same name, Millet, noting that he is not aware of any doctrinal prohibition against the display of crosses, suggests that perhaps the first Latter-day Saints did not use it largely because of their Puritan, anticonographic roots (105).[2] In addition, our cultural avoidance of focusing on Jesus's suffering in the hands of the Jewish and Roman authorities and his death upon the cross may also be a result of what Millet has called the tendency to "teach to our distinctives."[3] Because we have a deeper understanding of the role of Gethsemane in Jesus's saving work, we often focus on that critical part of the Atonement. To this I would add the human penchant to sometimes react against the teachings of others: because we feel that some of our friends of other Christian traditions overemphasize the cross, perhaps

we sometimes overcompensate by not considering it enough. Nevertheless, the cross is central to Jesus's own definition of what his gospel is. Speaking to the gathered Nephites, the Risen Lord proclaimed:

> And my Father sent me *that I might be lifted up upon the cross*; and after that I had been lifted up upon the cross, that I might draw all men unto me, *that as I have been lifted up by men even so should men be lifted up by the Father*, to stand before me, to be judged of their works, whether they be good or whether they be evil—
>
> And for this cause have I been lifted up; therefore, according to the power of the Father I will draw all men unto me, that they may be judged according to their works. (3 Nephi 27:14–15; emphasis added)

Jesus's Atoning Journey

The events between Gethsemane up to and including Golgotha are likewise important parts of our Atonement theology. Book of Mormon prophecies such as 1 Nephi 19:9, 2 Nephi 6:9, and Mosiah 3:9 emphasize how Jesus experienced betrayal, abandonment, rejection, abuse, and false judgment. No wife betrayed by a husband, no child abused by a parent, no friend rejected by another will fail to resonate with Jesus's being betrayed by the kiss of a friend, abandoned by his disciples, and denied, if only briefly, by Peter. No one who has ever been falsely judged can fail to relate to how Jesus, innocent and pure, was falsely accused and condemned. Through these experiences, Jesus "descended below all things" (D&C 88:6; see also D&C 122:8), and they may have been ways that Jesus shared such burdens.[4]

Reclaiming Good Friday and the cross thus begins, perhaps, by seeing Jesus's salvific work as an atoning *journey* rather than as a discrete event in the Garden of Gethsemane. Employing the Old Testament sacrificial model, this journey began when our burdens were placed upon Jesus in Gethsemane, just as an Israelite worshipper claimed his sacrificial victim by laying hands on it, symbolically transferring both ownership and guilt. It continued as Jesus was led away captive from the garden, carrying that burden, even as the scapegoat carried Israel's guilt. It culminated when he died upon the cross, just as a sin offering was slain for atonement or as the paschal lamb was slaughtered so that the sinful might live. And then, just as the smoke of the sacrifice rose to God, so did Jesus rise with newness of life through the Resurrection to ascend to his Father.[5]

This has led Elder Holland to "speak of the loneliest journey ever made and the unending blessings it brought to all in the human family. I speak of the Savior's solitary task of shouldering alone the burden of our salvation, . . . these scenes of Christ's lonely sacrifice, laced with moments of denial and abandonment and, at least once, outright betrayal."[6] Understanding that this journey includes betrayal, abandonment, denial, abuse, and false judgment provides poignant context for the well-known prophecy, "But he was wounded for our transgressions, he was bruised for our iniquities: the chastisement of our peace was upon him; and with his stripes we are healed" (Isaiah 53:5; cf. Mosiah 14:5).

Caravaggio, The Flagellation of Christ.

The "lifting up" motif of the Gospel according to John suggests that the importance of the cross is not its shape—which could have been a t-shaped *tau*, an x-shaped *chi*, something akin to the usually depicted Latin cross, or mere scaffolding or a convenient tree—not its later use in iconography.

To Nicodemus, Jesus declared, "And as Moses lifted up the serpent in the wilderness, even so must the Son of man be lifted up: that whosoever believeth in him should not perish, but have eternal life" (John 3:14–15). The type of the brazen serpent raised by Moses in Numbers 21:9 to provide healing for all who would look suggests that Jesus's being raised upon the cross was a symbol of how his atoning suffering and death are there for all to see and how he will heal all those who will look to him. To the Pharisees, he said, "When ye have lifted up the Son of man, then shall ye know that I am he" (John 8:28), and to the people before his Passion he prophesied, "And I, if I be lifted up from the earth, will draw all men unto me. This he said, signifying what death he should die" (John 12:32), words very close to what he would later use in 3 Nephi 27.[7]

Dying Daily in Christ

Another less-explored way of reclaiming the cross is to explore and embrace some of Paul's imagery and teaching, particularly "I protest by your rejoicing which I have in Christ Jesus our Lord, *I die daily*" (1 Corinthians 15:31; emphasis added). This concept of "dying daily" can be connected to the Pauline participation salvation model. Like many Latter-day leaders and teachers, the Apostle Paul strove to help explain the Atonement of Jesus Christ through different models or comparisons. Today we have President Packer's debtor model, President Gordon B. Hinckley's "He Took a Lickin' for Me" model, or Stephen Robinson's parable of the bicycle.[8] In his writings and those attributed to him, Paul employed a number of models including the judicial, rescue, expiation, and redemption models. Perhaps the most common, and important, is the reconciliation model, the Greek word *katallagē* for reconciliation also being the word translated as "atonement."[9] But of particular importance for the events of Good Friday is the participation model, which suggests that in some deep way we participate with Christ in the different aspects of his saving work, benefiting from their results and, sometimes, a degree of the experiences themselves.[10] It is in this way I suggest that we can understand Paul's references to dying with Christ.

First, Dying to Sin

In Romans 7:1–6, Paul uses an analogy from marriage to explain how Christians, especially Jewish Christians, were freed from the demands of the old law of Moses when they become new creatures in Christ. Just as a woman is free to remarry after her husband dies, so Christians are now party to a new covenant, the law of Christ. This has a possible illustration in a Jewish burial custom. Throughout an observant Jewish man's adult life, he wears a *tallit*, or fringed garment, as either a prayer shawl or *tallit gadol* for morning prayers and high holidays or as a special undergarment, the *tallit qatan*. Both have fringes that are tied in 613 knots, which represent the 613 *mitzvot* or commandments of the law. When a man dies, he may be wrapped in his *tallit*, the tassels of which are cut off to indicate that he is no longer bound by the law.[11]

Because both Romans and 2 Nephi 2 explain that one of the purposes of law is to define sin, the participation model

Tallit.

explains Paul's powerful baptismal imagery: "Know ye not, that so many of us as were baptized into Jesus Christ were baptized into his death? Therefore we are buried with him by

Garden Tomb.

baptism into death: that like as Christ was raised up from the
dead by the glory of the Father, even so we also should walk
in newness of life" (Romans 6:3–4). The old man or woman
of sin thus dies, emerging from the waters of baptism as a
new man or woman of Christ.[12] But as virtually all of us have
experienced, the mighty change of heart that we have at conversion does not always yield a permanent state of no longer
having a disposition to do evil, as King Benjamin describes it
(see Mosiah 5:2). Instead, most of us must frequently, even
daily, take personal inventory, asking ourselves with Alma, "If
ye have experienced a change of heart, and if ye have felt to

sing the song of redeeming love, I would ask, can ye feel so now?" (Alma 5:26). Having had that mighty change of heart and having been born of God—which are experiences so graphically illustrated by baptism—we must retain and often regain it, dying to sin daily and beginning to live in Christ anew. Is this partly what Paul meant when he said that he "died daily"?

Dying to Sorrow

On Good Friday, Jesus was the quintessential Man of Sorrows: "He is despised and rejected of men; a man of sorrows, and acquainted with grief. . . . Surely he hath borne our griefs, and carried our sorrows: yet we did esteem him stricken, smitten of God, and afflicted" (Isaiah 53:3–4). I came to better understand this right before Easter in 2007. Our son, Samuel, was just being diagnosed with Autism Spectrum Disorder, and our hearts were broken. Already suffering from a developmental delay, our little boy stopped smiling, rarely talked, and would not look at us in the eye or let us hold him. On the Thursday before Easter while in the Provo Utah Temple, I poured my heart out to the Lord in the celestial room. I felt words and phrases come into my mind in response to each of my silent pleas. When I expressed my sadness that my son might not have all the traditional opportunities and life experiences that LDS parents often expect for their children—such as serving a conventional, full-time mission and marrying in the temple—the answer that came was direct. Many young men and women in the Church do not have those opportunities, the Spirit seemed to say, but

Eric and Samuel Huntsman.

often it is because of choices they make. If Samuel did not, it was because he was not able, and he would not be deprived of any blessing in the eternities. Understanding but still distraught, I cried out in my heart, "But Lord, he is my only son!" As chance had it, that day was Maundy Thursday, the Thursday before Easter that commemorates the Last Supper and Jesus's suffering in Gethsemane. The next day was Good Friday, when the Son of God suffered and died for all of us. The clear response to my cry was firm and struck me to the core: "What about my Only Son?"

In the years since, we have seen miracles small and great in Samuel's life. He is mainstreamed in public school, and last year I ordained him a deacon. He smiles, talks, and laughs. There are still disappointments, challenges, and heartaches, but I am learning to allow sorrow to draw me closer to my

Savior. How often do we pray, asking the Lord to make us more like Jesus? Then, when the trials and heartaches come that will refine and shape us, we more often than not plea for him to take them away. There is something about suffering with Jesus that makes us more like him. And if this is true, then "death," both actual and metaphorical, can signal the end of suffering. Alma taught, "And then shall it come to pass, that the spirits of those who are righteous are received into a state of happiness, which is called paradise, a state of rest, a state of peace, *where they shall rest from all their troubles and from all care, and sorrow*" (Alma 40:12; emphasis added). Jesus bore our griefs and carried them to the cross. When our sorrows bring us closer to Jesus, the miracle of the Atonement is that he lifts them, carries them, and dies for them. Trusting Christ, availing ourselves of his comforting grace, means letting the man or woman of sorrow die each day.

Dying to Sickness and Infirmity

One of the great Christological contributions of the Book of Mormon is found in Alma's sermon in Gideon. Apparently drawing upon Isaiah 53:4, as Matthew later would, Alma prophesied, "And he shall go forth, suffering pains and afflictions and temptations of every kind; and this that the word might be fulfilled which saith he will take upon him the pains and the sicknesses of his people. . . . He will take upon him their infirmities, that his bowels may be filled with mercy, according to the flesh, that he may know according to the flesh how to succor his people according to their infirmities" (Alma 7:11–12; Matthew 8:16–17). In addition to taking upon himself our sins and

Eric and Marilyn Huntsman.

our sorrows, here Alma teaches us that Jesus also bears our pains, sicknesses, and weaknesses. From this arises our understanding of the beautiful healing power of Christ's grace.

In our mortal lives we often describe death as bringing welcome relief to pain and sickness. Indeed, how often do we speak of someone who dies after a long illness by observing, "Well, at least he is no longer suffering." This was the case with my own dear mother. A three-time cancer survivor, she endured to the end, living life as fully as she could, serving her family and her church with faith and an inspiring, positive attitude. Finally, however, Mother's body, ravaged by cancer treatments, at last faltered in the face of renal and then heart failure. In her final months, this once vibrant, joyful woman literally withered before our eyes. As heart-wrenching as her death was to me, when she passed peacefully in my home with me standing by her side and my daughter holding my hand, I felt to thank God that her struggle was over and that she was no longer in pain. Seeing the peaceful expression on her face, I knew that her spirit was now free.

Following Paul, I would suggest that Jesus did not just vicariously suffer for our infirmities, but he took them up and carried them to the cross, where his death brought them to an end. Even as Jesus heals our hearts of sorrow, so he can heal our bodies, miraculously in this life and ultimately through the Resurrection. The mortal man and woman of sickness and death can be strengthened and sustained in this life and ultimately exchange this corruption for incorruption.

The Lamb of God

To the Pauline concept of our sin, sorrows, and infirmities being swallowed up in the death of Christ, I would add one other powerful Johannine image. This is of Jesus as the Lamb of God who "taketh away the sin of the world" (John 1:29). Significantly, "sin" here is in the singular, referring apparently not only to our individual sins and transgressions but more broadly to our sinful, fallen, and mortal state. Indeed, I would suggest that in John, Jesus's saving death is portrayed primarily as the source of spiritual, eternal life. Whereas the synoptics largely employ the imagery of Jesus's death as a sacrificial offering for sin, the blood of the first Passover lambs was intended to ward off death and allow new life. Even as that blood was spread on the wooden door frames of the huts of the Hebrews in Egypt, now the blood of the Lamb of God stained the wood of the cross. Not only did Jesus's death on the cross ward off spiritual death, the water that flowed with the blood from his side can symbolize a fountain of life-giving water springing up unto everlasting life.

Indeed, part of reclaiming the cross is seeing it not just as a symbol of death but as a source of new life. This is illustrated in the legend—perhaps better the allegory—of Adam's tomb. In the Middle Ages arose the story that Adam had been buried under Golgotha. Thus, in the Church of

Francisco de Zurbarán, "Agnus Dei."

the Holy Sepulchre under the Greek and Latin altars of Calvary lies the Chapel of Adam, with a pane of glass revealing the rock of Golgotha. Thus, when Jesus later died upon the cross, the blood and water from his side ran down its post and flowed into Adam's grave, making him the first beneficiary of Christ's saving blood and life-giving stream. While this is but a legend, it speaks to the truth that "for as in Adam all die, even so in Christ shall all be made alive" (1 Corinthians 15:22). This also gave rise to the image of the Verdant Cross, a cross that sprouted leaves and fruit. In other words, the dead tree of cursing had become a new tree of life.

72

Commonly, we explain our wariness of the cross by emphasizing that we worship a living Christ, not a dying Jesus. It is true that our Catholic friends utilize a crucifix—that is, a depiction of Jesus on the cross—largely for liturgical reasons, because the celebration of each mass is a new sacrifice. But I remember being surprised once when a former Presbyterian friend corrected me when I told her that we preferred to worship a living rather than a dead Christ; she responded that she did too. The cross reminded Protestants that Jesus died for their sins, but it was empty because he was risen and was no longer there on it. I was chastened by her response, realizing that just as we do not appreciate others mischaracterizing our beliefs, neither should we presume to understand or misrepresent the beliefs and practices of others.

While President Hinckley taught that the lives of our people—lives transformed by Christ—are the most meaningful expressions of our faith and serve as the symbol of our

Matt Reier, Nails. © *Intellectual Reserve, Inc.*

Pacino di Bonaguida, Tree of Life.

worship, he also said, "No member of this Church must ever forget the terrible price paid by our Redeemer, who gave his life that all men might live . . . This was the cross on which he hung and died on Golgotha's lonely summit. We cannot forget that. We must never forget it, for here our Savior, our Redeemer, the Son of God, gave himself a vicarious sacrifice for each of us."[13]

And so while I, with you, look forward with eager anticipation to the joy of Easter morning, and while I live each day with a firm assurance that he lives, on Good Friday I pause to think of his suffering and death. Tonight in Salt Lake some 360 of my closest friends will be closing their performance of Handel's *Messiah* with the words of the heavenly hosts, singing, "Worthy is the Lamb that was slain, and hath redeemed us to God by his blood, to receive power, and riches, and wisdom, and strength, and honour, and glory, and blessing. . . . Blessing and honour, glory and power, be unto him that sitteth upon the throne, and unto the Lamb, for ever and ever" (Revelation 5:12–13).

Thanks be to God, who has given us this victory through Jesus Christ, our Lord. I know that he took upon himself our sins, sorrows, and weaknesses in Gethsemane and carried them to the cross. I know that he suffered and died for me and for you. I know that he came forth from the tomb that first Easter, rising with healing in his wings. May we stand as witnesses of this at all times, in all things, and in all places—preaching Jesus Christ, and him crucified and risen.

Notes

1. Gaye Strathearn, "Christ's Crucifixion: Reclamation of the Cross," *Religious Educator* 14, no. 1 (2013): 45–57.

2. Robert L. Millet, "What Happened to the Cross?," in *What Happened to the Cross?* (Salt Lake City: Deseret Book, 2007), 105.

3. Millet, "What Happened to the Cross?," 106–7.

4. Eric D. Huntsman, *God So Loved the World* (Salt Lake City: Deseret Book, 2011), 66.

5. Huntsman, *God So Loved the World*, 66.

6. Jeffery R. Holland, "None Were with Him," *Ensign*, May 2009, 86.

7. Leon Morris, *The Gospel according to John* (Grand Rapids, MI: Eerdmans, 1995), 198–99, 401, 531–32; Huntsman, *God So Loved the World*, 84–85.

8. Boyd K. Packer, "The Mediator," *Ensign*, May 1977, 54–55; Gordon B. Hinckley, "The Wondrous and True Story of Christmas," *Ensign*, December 2000, 4; Stephen E. Robinson, *Believing Christ* (Salt Lake City: Deseret Book, 1992), 30–32.

9. James D. G. Dunn, *The Theology of Paul the Apostle* (Grand Rapids, MI: Eerdmans, 1998), 212–23, 227–31.

10. Dunn, *Theology of Paul*, 482–87.

11. Hayim Halevy Donim, *To Be a Jew* (New York: Basic Books, 1972), 297.

12. See the discussion of Douglas J. Moo, *The Epistle to the Romans*, The New International Commentary on the New Testament (Grand Rapids, MI: Eerdmans, 1996), 359–69.

13. Gordon B. Hinckley, "The Symbol of Faith," *Ensign*, April 2005, 4.

NEW CREATURES
IN CHRIST

Daniel K Judd

Daniel K Judd is a professor of ancient scripture at BYU.

The Book of Mormon prophet Alma taught the people of Gideon, "There be many things to come; and behold, there is one thing which is of more importance than they all—for behold, the time is not far distant that the Redeemer liveth and cometh among his people" (Alma 7:7). In addition to the many blessings that have come to humankind through the mortal ministry and life of Jesus Christ, prophets, both ancient and modern, have also explained the eternal significance of the Savior's death and Resurrection. President Howard W. Hunter taught the following: "The doctrine of the Resurrection is the single most fundamental and crucial doctrine in the Christian religion. It cannot be overemphasized, nor can it be disregarded. Without the Resurrection, the gospel of Jesus Christ becomes a litany of wise sayings

Simon Dewey

and seemingly unexplainable miracles."[1] While the general purpose of this chapter is to review the historical and doctrinal significance of the Atonement and Resurrection of Jesus Christ, the specific intent is to serve as an invitation for us as individuals, families, and a community of believers to continue our journey in becoming, in the words of the Apostle Paul, "new creatures" (see 2 Corinthians 5:17), even new creatures in Christ.

The process of becoming men and women of Christ (see 3 Nephi 27:27) often includes inspired thoughts and feelings that come to both heart and mind. Many years ago when I was serving as a young missionary, my companion and I were teaching a young couple about the principle of restitution as a part of the process of repentance. As we were discussing the importance of doing "all we can do" (2 Nephi 25:23) to make the appropriate restitution for the sins in our lives, I began to feel uneasy as I remembered a poor choice I had made several years earlier for which I had never made amends. I also sensed the hypocrisy of asking this couple to live a principle that I was not fully living myself. When I was twelve years old, I stole a copy of *Sport Magazine* from a store in my hometown of Kanab, Utah, for which I had never made any attempt at restitution. After taking some time to think about what I had done and what I could do to make things right, I decided to write a letter of apology to Neil Crosby, the owner of Kanab Drug. Brother Crosby was also my neighbor and a member of the Kanab North Ward, the ward in which I had been born into and grown up in as a young man. In addition to my apology and asking Brother Crosby's forgiveness, I included a check for fifteen dollars to cover the cost of the magazine I had stolen and to make up for the interest that had accrued in the intervening years.

Imagine my surprise when I received a letter from Brother Crosby a few weeks later that read something like this, "Dear Elder Judd, thank you for your letter and for your apology; I forgive you." His letter continued, "I remember how disappointed I was the night I watched you take that magazine from my store without paying, but I always hoped the day would come when you would make it right." In addition to the letter, Brother Crosby had returned my check and also included a check he had made out to me for fifty dollars. He finished his letter by thanking me for my honesty and wishing me continued success on my mission. While some would say that I "made money" on that particular sin, a more inspired response would be to express gratitude for the support of a good neighbor, and even more importantly, the grace and mercy of a loving God and the promise that he will "consecrate [our] afflictions" and even our sins "for [our] gain" (2 Nephi 2:2) as we approach him with "a broken heart and a contrite spirit" (2 Nephi 2:7).

Many years later, one of my missionaries with whom I was serving in West Africa asked me an interesting question after listening to the story I have just shared with you. "President," the missionary asked, "is sin something we must experience to receive the full blessings of the atonement of Christ?" While I chose to answer the missionary's question by reading from the writings of the Apostle Paul to the Romans (see Romans 6:1–2), the question has an interesting history.

In the early part of the twentieth century, there was a Russian mystic and self-described prophet by the name of

Grigori Rasputin, whose false teachings on grace along with his reported licentious behavior have been identified by some scholars as a contributing factor to the corruption of the administration of Tsar Nicholas II of Russia and the downfall of the Romanov Dynasty.[2] Rasputin taught that "without sin there is no life, because there is no repentance, and if there is no repentance, there is no joy."[3] Rasputin's assertion that one should sin as a means of experiencing God's grace gained a following of those who embraced his distorted doctrine. Sadly, Rasputin's life embodied what is described in the Epistle of Jude as "ungodly men, turning the grace of our Lord into lasciviousness" (Jude 1:4).

The Apostle Paul's answer to Rasputin's gross immorality and my missionary's honest question is found in the sixth chapter of Romans when Paul asked the rhetorical question, "Shall we continue in sin, that grace may abound?" Paul's emphatic reply was, "*God forbid*. How shall we, that are dead to sin, live any longer therein?" (Romans 6:1–2). In addition to his passionate warning against sin, Paul is also teaching the principle that once our hearts are truly changed, we, in the words of the Zarahemla Saints, "have no more disposition to do evil, but to do good continually" (Mosiah 5:2). This isn't to say that after experiencing this "mighty change" (Alma 5:12) we won't ever sin again, but when we have experienced a change of heart, both our motives and actions change. Note the doctrinal contrast between the King James and Joseph Smith Translations of 1 John 3:8–9.

The scriptural phrases in the King James Version that read "He that committeth sin is of the devil" and "Whosoever is born of God doth not commit sin . . ." can be discouraging for those of us who are diligently striving to keep the commandments but who still fall from time to time. The King James Version implies that once a person is born again, they will never sin. The Joseph Smith Translation of the same texts reads, "He that continueth in sin is of the devil" and "Whosoever is born of God doth not continue in sin" (JST, 1 John 3:8–9). From the JST we learn that faithful people sin, but they honestly strive to repent and not continue to transgress the laws of God.

King James Version	Joseph Smith Translation
8 He that **committeth sin is of the devil; for the devil** sinneth from the beginning. For this purpose the Son of God was manifested, that he might destroy the works of the devil.	8 He that **continueth** in sin is of the devil; for the devil sinneth from the beginning. For this purpose the Son of God was manifested, that he might destroy the works of the devil.
9 **Whosoever is born of God doth not commit sin**; for his seed remaineth in him: and he cannot sin, because he is born of God. (1 John 3:8–9)	9 Whosoever is born of God doth not **continue** in sin; for the Spirit of God remaineth in him; and he cannot **continue** in sin, because he is born of God . . . (1 John 3:9–9)

Elder Dallin H. Oaks taught the following to those who believe that they are better off to have sinned and repented than never to have sinned at all: "Some Latter-day Saints who think repentance is easy, maintain that a person is better off after he has sinned and repented. 'Get a little experience with sin,' one argument goes, 'and then you will be better able to counsel others and sympathize with others. Anyway, it won't hurt to sin a little.'" Elder Oaks continued: "I plead with you, my brothers and sisters, my young friends and my older friends, avoid transgression! The idea that one is better off after one has sinned and repented is a devilish lie of the adversary."[4]

After the Apostle Paul's emphatic response, "God forbid," to his question about whether we should deliberately sin in order to experience God's grace, he continued his explanation by asking another of his seventy-four rhetorical questions[5] included in the Epistle to the Romans: "Know ye not," Paul asked, "that so many of us as were baptized into Jesus Christ were baptized into his death?" (Romans 6:3). What is Paul asking by inviting us to be "baptized into Jesus Christ" and to be "baptized into [Christ's] death? Paul's answer to these question leads us to a greater understanding of the Savior's death and Resurrection: Paul answered:

> Therefore we are buried with him by baptism into death: that like as Christ was raised up from the dead by the glory of the Father, even so we also should walk in newness of life.
>
> For if we have been planted together in the likeness of his death, we shall be also in the likeness of his resurrection:
>
> Knowing this, that our old man is crucified with him, that the body of sin might be destroyed, that henceforth we should not serve sin. (Romans 6:4–6)

Paul is using the literal death and Resurrection of Jesus Christ as symbolic representations to invite the reader to put to death the natural man within each of us, through faith in Christ, repentance, and baptism, that we may come forth as "new creature[s]" (2 Corinthians 5:17) in Christ to sin no more. British pastor and theologian Charles Spurgeon (1834–92) gave the following illustration of what it means to repent and to be "baptized unto [Christ's] death" and become a "new creature in Christ." While the original source for the story can't be identified, Spurgeon believed the story is from the life of St. Augustine, the fourth-century bishop in northern Africa: "Augustine had indulged in great sins in his younger days. After his conversion he met with a woman who had been the sharer of his wicked follies; she approached him winningly and said to him . . . 'Augustine, it is I,' mentioning her name; but [Augustine] then turned round and said, 'But it is not I;

Augustine, AD 354 – AD 430. Charles Spurgeon, Spurgeon's Sermons, 19:353.

the old Augustine is dead and I am a new creature in Christ Jesus.'"[6]

As each of us strives to repent of our sins and be "buried with [Christ] by baptism into death" and is blessed to "walk in newness of life" (Romans 6:4), we join with other disciples from the beginning of time as witnesses of the Atonement, death, and the Resurrection of the Savior.

The infinite Atonement of Jesus Christ makes this change possible, and has meaning for each of us no matter the degree or nature of our sins. President Boyd K. Packer taught, "Save for those few who defect to perdition after having known a fulness, there is no habit, no addiction, no rebellion, no transgression, no offense exempted from the promise of complete forgiveness." In the same conference address, President Packer continued by describing the connection between our sins, small and great, and the Atonement of Christ:

> When an offense is minor, so simple a thing as an apology will satisfy the law. Most mistakes can be settled between us and the Lord, and that should be done speedily (see D&C 109:21). It requires a confession to Him, and whatever obvious repairs need to be made. . .
>
> To earn forgiveness, one must make restitution. That means you give back what you have taken or ease the pain of those you have injured. But sometimes you cannot give back what you have taken because you don't have it to give. If you have caused others to suffer unbearably, . . . it is not within your power to give it back.
>
> There are times you cannot mend that which you have broken. Perhaps the offense was long ago, or the injured refused your penance. Perhaps the damage was so severe that you cannot fix it no matter how desperately you want to.

President Packer concludes his remarkable statement by describing the purpose and power of the Atonement of Jesus Christ:

Restoring what you cannot restore, healing the wound you cannot heal, *fixing that which you broke and you cannot fix is the very purpose of the atonement of Christ.*

When your desire is firm and you are willing to pay the "uttermost farthing" (see Matthew 5:25–26) the law of restitution is suspended. Your obligation is transferred to the Lord. He will settle your accounts.[7]

There are sins in our lives that have been or continue to be a part of us for which we could not or cannot make full restitution. There are also other problems we have in our personal lives, in the lives of our family members, for which we do not have the solution. A careful study of the teachings of the Savior and his servants reveal that these too, in the words of Abinadi, may be "swallowed up in Christ" (Mosiah 16:8) as we remain faithful to the sacred covenants we have made.

When confronted with the reality of sin, some of us deceive ourselves into believing that we are not guilty, or we may even come to believe there is no such thing as sin (see 2 Nephi 2:13). Sometimes we use the sins of others to justify our own. Amulek, reflecting on his own state of self-deception, stated: "I was called many times and I would not hear; therefore I knew concerning these things, yet I would not know" (Alma 10:6). Others fall into despair, what the Apostle Paul describes as "overmuch sorrow" (2 Corinthians 2:7) believing that their sins or other problems are beyond the redeeming power of Christ. One such individual who suffered from such feelings of despair is the Protestant reformer Martin Luther.

When Luther was twenty-one years old, he entered the Augustinian monastery in Erfurt, Germany, to begin

Lucas Cranach the Elder, Martin Luther *(1528).*

his training to become a priest. By his own account and the records of his peers, Luther was an exceptional and dedicated monk. His first year went well, but as his training progressed, he began to experience feelings of anxiety and despair. Luther did what many of us do when we experience such problems: he began to work harder, striving to be more faithful. Sadly (but instructively), instead of gaining strength, his depression and anxiety increased. In Luther's own words, we read:

When I was a monk, I made a great effort to live according to the requirements of the monastic rule. I made a practice of confessing and reciting all my sins, but always with prior contrition; I went to confession frequently, and I performed the assigned penances faithfully. Nevertheless, my conscience could never achieve certainty but was always in doubt and said: "You have not done this correctly. You were not contrite enough. You omitted this in your confession." Therefore, the longer I tried to heal my uncertain, weak, and troubled conscience with human traditions, the more uncertain, weak, and troubled I continually made it. In this way, by observing human traditions, I transgressed them even more; and by following the righteousness of the monastic order, I was never able to reach it.[8]

My clinical training and pastoral experience led me to believe, after reading much of what Luther wrote during his years in the monastery, that his emotional problems didn't originate with sin, but were more psychological, doctrinal, and perhaps physiological in nature. The good news for Martin Luther, and for all of humankind, is that the Atonement of Christ isn't just for those guilty of sin, the Savior's sufferings are also for those who, in the words of the Book of Mormon prophet Alma, suffer "pains and afflictions and temptations of every kind" (Alma 7:11), including what King Benjamin described as "infirmities in body and mind" (Mosiah 2:11).

For ten years, Luther labored with increasing feelings of guilt, doubt, and compulsivity without finding relief. It wasn't until after his leaders became frustrated with him and transferred him to Wittenberg University to pursue a

Grace and Mental Health

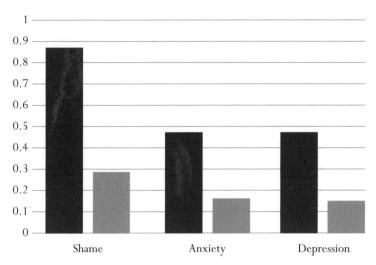

Daniel K Judd, W. Justin Dyer, & Justin B. Top, "Relationships among Grace and Mental Health: A Structural Equation Model," Advances in the Measurement of Religion and Spirituality. Symposium conducted at the meeting of the American Psychological Association, New York City, March 2016.

Doctor of Divinity degree and he started to teach the Bible that Luther finally began, through diligent study and teaching of scripture, to find peace, or more precisely, the Prince of Peace, Jesus Christ.

Luther's rediscovery of the grace of Christ was a key moment in the history of Christianity and was a major factor in preparing for the restored gospel. Elder Bruce R. McConkie described Luther's work as "an Elias preparing the way for the Restoration."[9]

While many have identified Luther's dissatisfaction with the sixteenth-century Catholic Church's sale of indulgences as being the catalyst that brought about the Protestant Reformation, I believe and have described at some length in an academic paper addressing the issue that while religious legalism was certainly a factor, a far more compelling dynamic was Luther's own legalism related to his psychological concerns and spiritual insecurity.[10]

In March of 2016, my colleagues and I presented a paper at a conference of the American Psychological Association in Brooklyn, New York. We discussed the life of Luther and our findings of a recent study we conducted with 574 Brigham Young University students with respect to their experience with legalism, grace, and various measures of mental health. We found that the more the respondents believed that their salvation was primarily a result of their own good works (legalism), the higher were their scores on measures of shame, anxiety, depression, and obsessive-compulsive behavior (scrupulosity). When we examined the influence of grace with these same students, we found that those who understood and embraced the principle of grace had dramatically lower scores on these same measures.[11]

The following statement from Elder M. Russell Ballard warns of the dangers of becoming preoccupied with good works and not learning to embrace the grace of Christ:

> No matter how hard we work, no matter how much we obey, no matter how many good things we do in this life, it would not be enough were it not for Jesus Christ and His loving grace. On our own we cannot earn the kingdom of God—no matter what we do. Unfortunately, there are some within the Church who have become so preoccupied with

performing good works that they forget that those works—
as good as they may be—are hollow unless they are accompanied by a complete dependence on Christ.[12]

Many of us first experience the goodness and grace of God when our sins have driven us to our knees and we have no other place to turn. Others come discover the Savior through afflictions of a different kind. In addition to the profound discourse from the prophet Alma mentioned earlier (see Alma 7:11–16), modern prophets have also taught that the Atonement of Jesus Christ is also for all who experience pain and affliction associated with physical and emotional concerns. While many of our prophet leaders have taught this hopeful doctrine, my first recollection of what has come to be known as the enabling or strengthening power of the Savior's Atonement was taught by Elder Neal A. Maxwell in general conference in April of 1985. Elder Maxwell's words are as follows: "The cumulative weight of all mortal sins— past, present, and future—pressed upon that perfect, sinless, and sensitive Soul! *All our infirmities and sicknesses were somehow, too, a part of the awful arithmetic of the Atonement.*[13] Elder Maxwell would later write, "Since not all human sorrow and pain is connected to sin, the full intensiveness of the Atonement involved bearing our pains, infirmities, and sicknesses, as well as our sins. Whatever our sufferings, we can safely cast our "care upon him; for he careth for [us]" (1 Peter 5:7).[14]

While I have been blessed throughout my life to serve and to work in various capacities that have allowed me to observe both the redemptive and strengthening blessings of the Atonement of Jesus Christ from a variety of perspectives, the three years Sister Judd and I lived in Ghana, West Africa, helped us understand God's love for his children and our love for him in a different way.

The people of Africa have been described as having "very little of that which matters least and a great deal of that which matters most."[15] One of the many expressions of "what matters most" to many Africans is found in a phrase that is common to most conversations and is also observed in the names people give their businesses and even on the windows of taxicabs and buses.

The phrase "by his grace" is common to the language of the rich and poor, educated and illiterate, the whole and the disabled. The African people acknowledge the sovereignty and graciousness of God. Rarely do they ask, "why" but most always "how can my life glorify God?"

One of our sister missionaries, Sister Lydia Abbot, joined the Church in Uganda when she was an adult, but escaped from her family and the jail in which her eldest brother had placed her when she announced that she was going on a mission. Her brother, once a bitter enemy of the Church, was eventually baptized and is now serving in a branch presidency—by his grace.

Elder Derrick Bagazwaga left a militant rebel army in Northern Uganda in which he was a soldier after hearing the restored gospel taught for the first time. After returning from serving his mission in Ghana, he is now preparing to marry his branch president's daughter—by the grace of God.

Eric Orlando, who currently serves as the chief auditor of the Supreme Court of Ghana, was baptized in the face of considerable political and family pressure. He would later

The phrase "By His Grace" is ever-present.

assist the Church's legal department in securing the land for continued use of the Accra Ghana Temple. He has also been instrumental in beginning a branch of the Church in his native village—by his grace.

The head of immigration at Ghana's International Airport was baptized after being visited by his deceased father in a dream. When his father was alive, he had often warned his family not to look at the Latter-day Saint temple in Accra as they would drive by or they would be cursed. In the dream (which he experienced three different times on three successive nights), the father apologized for what he had told his son about the Latter-day Saints and instructed him to go to the same temple and be baptized for him as soon as possible. The son went to the temple and asked how he could baptize

Sister Kaye Judd and two children

from the Kpong Branch.

his father even though he was dead. The man was informed that he would first need to be baptized himself. He was later baptized (as was his father), along with his wife, who is the chief officer for British Airways in Ghana. Her conversion began in large part by observing the "mighty change" (Alma 5:12) her husband experienced by embracing the restored gospel— by his grace.

Several of my missionaries were born into countries in the midst of civil war. These courageous elders and sisters from Sierra Leone, Liberia, and South Sudan have found peace, hope, and stability. These missionaries know they have a loving Father. They have faith in Jesus Christ and his Atonement and are striving to learn and to follow the language of revelation through the Holy Ghost. They sustain our living prophets. The restored gospel has made all the difference—by his grace.

Missionaries travel to Ghana from Western countries and learn to wash their clothes in a bucket. They live in difficult circumstances including contracting malaria and a host of other diseases that sometimes lasts for the duration of their missions and beyond. They quickly learn to love the people,

Missionaries in the Ghana Accra Mission, Christmas 2013.

the Lord, the Savior's servants, and his Church—by his grace. My eternal missionary companion, Sister Judd, while suffering with a serious illness has also been blessed with remarkable peace, good humor, and stability—by his grace.

Missionaries from fifty-four different countries came together in a common cause to preach the restored gospel of Jesus Christ. There was very little racial or cultural tension as they learned to feast upon the words of Christ in the Book of Mormon. They learned to work hard, work smart, and to love the Lord and those they teach—by his grace.

Through the strengthening and enabling influence of the Savior, the good and meaningful lives these returned missionaries are living are testimonies of the living reality of the life, Atonement, death, and Resurrection of the Lord Jesus Christ.

Counterfeits

With all of the beauty and power of the redemptive and strengthening dimensions of the Atonement of Christ, there are, however, cautions. President Ezra Taft Benson taught, "Whenever the God of heaven reveals His gospel to mankind, Satan, the archenemy to Christ, introduces a counterfeit."[16] As has already been mentioned, the counterfeit of obedience and good works is known as "legalism," the idea that we must earn a place in heaven by our personal righteousness. This is the false doctrine the prophet Lehi was addressing when he taught his son Jacob, "By the law no flesh is justified" (2 Nephi 2:5). The Apostle Paul, whose life as a Pharisee had been consumed with the law, taught, "For by grace are ye saved through faith; and that not of yourselves: it is the gift of God: not of works, lest any man should boast" (Ephesians 2:8–9).

The doctrine of grace also has a deceptive counterfeit. The technical term is "antinomianism," but this counterfeit is better known by the term "cheap grace." German theologian and pastor Dietrich Bonhoeffer warned, "Cheap grace is preaching forgiveness without repentance; it is baptism without the discipline of community; it is the Lord's Supper without confession of sin; it is absolution without personal confession. Cheap grace is grace without discipleship, grace without the cross, grace without the living, incarnate Jesus Christ."[17]

Cheap grace is the counterfeit the Apostle James was addressing when he stated, "Faith, if it hath not works, is dead, being alone" (James 2:17). While it is true that Martin Luther called the book of James an "epistle of straw"[18] because of what James had taught about the necessity of good works, there were other times Luther cautioned about the dangers of taking both good works or grace beyond what the Lord intended. Luther recorded, "Both groups, sin against the Law: those on the right, who want to be justified through the Law, and those on the left, who want to be altogether free of the Law. Therefore, we must travel the royal road, so that we neither reject the Law altogether nor attribute more to it than we should."[19]

Conclusion

Becoming "new creatures" in Christ requires both his grace and our faith. Genuine faith in Christ is manifest in our obedience to his law, because his law is a manifestation of who he is. The Savior taught the ancient Nephites, "Behold, I am the law, and the light. Look unto me, and endure to the end, and ye shall live; for unto him that endureth to the end will I give eternal life" (3 Nephi 15:9). I remember sitting with a missionary who was demanding to return home early from his mission. He didn't have any health concerns or worthiness issues that would justify him returning home, but he was convinced that he didn't want to be a missionary.

He was a convert from Islam of just a few years and had made great personal sacrifices to embrace Christianity, be baptized, and come on a mission. "President," he said,

"I want to go home, and there is nothing you can say that will change my mind." I responded by saying, "Elder, I want to go home too." I explained to him that my daughter Jessi was being sealed in the Provo Utah Temple later that week, and I wasn't going to be there. This sweet, wonderful elder then began to comfort me. He explained to me that I was the mission president and that I couldn't go home; the missionaries loved and needed me. We both began to shed a few tears as we shared our sorrows. We read together the Savior's words as he knelt in the Garden of Gethsemane: "Father, if thou be willing, remove this cup from me: nevertheless not my will, but thine, be done" (Luke 22:42). Like the Savior, we too felt angels "strengthening" us (Luke 22:43) as we made the decision that it was our Father's will that we stay and work together to bless those whom we had been sent to serve. The elder remained in the mission field and fulfilled a wonderful mission. That night, both of us came a little closer to becoming the men our Father in Heaven would have us be, even "new creatures" in Christ— by his grace.

Notes

1. Howard W. Hunter, "An Apostle's Witness of the Resurrection," *Ensign*, May 1986, 15.

2. R. Kent Hughes, *Romans: Righteousness from Heaven* (Wheaton, IL: Crossway Books, 1991), 121.

3. Grigori Rasputin, as quoted in Edvard Radzinsky, *The Rasputin File* (New York: Anchor Books, 2001), 240.

4. Dallin H. Oaks, "Sin and Suffering," in *Morality* (Salt Lake City: Deseret Book, 1992), 190.

5. Bruce Kaye, *The Argument of Romans with Special Reference to Chapter 6* (Austin, TX: Scholars Press, 1979), 14.

6. Charles H. Spurgeon, *Spurgeon's Sermons*, 19:353 (Kindle Edition).

7. Boyd K. Packer, "The Brilliant Morning of Forgiveness," *Ensign*, November 1995, 19–20; emphasis added.

8. Martin Luther, in *Luther's Works*, ed. Jaroslav Pelikan (St. Louis: Concordia Publishing House, 1955), 27:13.

9. Bruce R. McConkie, *Sermons and Writings of Bruce R. McConkie*, ed. Mark L. McConkie (Salt Lake City: Deseret Book, 1989), 72.

10. Daniel K Judd, "Clinical and Pastoral Implications of the Ministry of Martin Luther and the Protestant Reformation," *Open Theology* 2, no. 1 (2016): 324–37.

11. Daniel K Judd and W. Justin Dyer, "Relationships Among Grace, Legalism, and Mental Health in an LDS Sample: A Structural Equation Model" (forthcoming paper).

12. M. Russell Ballard, "Building Bridges of Understanding," *Ensign*, June 1998, 65.

13. Neal A. Maxwell, "Willing to Submit," *Ensign*, May 1985, 73; emphasis added.

14. Neal A. Maxwell, *Not My Will, But Thine* (Salt Lake City: Deseret Book, 1988), 51.

15. John B. Dickson, "The Gospel to All the World," *Ensign*, May 2013, 41.

16. Ezra Taft Benson, *A Witness and a Warning*, *Ensign*, November 1979, 31.

17. Dietrich Bonhoeffer, *Discipleship*, ed. M. Kuske et al., trans. B. Green and R. Krauss (Minneapolis, MN: Fortress Press, 2003), 4:44.

18. Martin Luther, *Luther's Works*, ed. J. J. Pelikan, H. C. Oswald, and H. T. Lehmann (Philadelphia: Fortress Press, 1999), 35:362.

19. Martin Luther, *Luther's Works*, 27:13.

A NEW COMMANDMENT

The Transformative Power of Redeeming Love

Camille Fronk Olson

*Camille Fronk Olson is a professor of ancient
scripture at Brigham Young University.*

Before the scourging and the cross was Gethsemane. And
before Gethsemane was the Last Supper. In an upper
room that Jesus preselected (see Luke 22:7–13 and Mark
14:12–16), he created an environment to poignantly communicate the importance of what was about happen to him
that would enable the gift of eternal salvation and blessings in
mortality for all of humankind.

In a testimony addressed to deeply converted followers of
Jesus Christ, the Apostle John devoted one-fourth of his entire
Gospel, five of twenty-one chapters (John 13–17), to events and
teachings that occurred during or shortly after the Last Supper.

Leonardo da Vinci, The Last Supper.

Previously, Jesus had reminded his followers that his "hour" was not yet come. His hour was neither at the time he turned water into wine in Cana (see John 2:4), neither at a previous Passover when many in Jerusalem wanted to kill him (see John 7:8), nor when he taught in the temple treasury, "that knowing him was akin to knowing the Father and they wanted to kill him" (John 8:19–20). Now, with the fourth and final feast of the Passover marking his ministry approaching, he "knew that his hour was come that he should depart out of this world unto the Father, having loved his own which went in the world, he loved them unto the end" (John 13:1). Here in this upper room, he prepared to show his perfect love, poured out through action and word, a harbinger of the infinite redeeming love he would pour out through pain and agony during the next twenty-four hours.

In this upper-room setting, Jesus gave them "a new commandment" that requires a change in the way we see each other and the way we reverence him. He explained, "That ye love one another; as I have loved you. . . . By this shall all men know that ye are my disciples, if ye have love one to another" (John 13:34–35). I want to explore how obedience to this new commandment is at the heart of our being changed forever through the Atonement of Jesus Christ. By serious consideration of how Jesus illustrated and described how we learn to love others as he loves them, we may choose to progress along this transformative spiritual journey. Specifically, I will focus on Jesus washing the feet of the Twelve in John 13, his imagery of us as branches on the true vine in John 15, and the culmination of the upper-room experience, when he prayed to the Father that we be made "one" as the Father is in him and as he is in the Father (John 17:21).

Washing Feet

In what must have been a surprise to the Twelve, Jesus arose during the supper to wash their feet.[1] Hosts often provided water for guests to pour over their feet when they first arrived to their home or right before they dined, but seeing the *host* washing the guests' feet and *during* a meal would have been wholly unexpected.

The text indicates that what Jesus would do next was purposeful and in full awareness of his role as the Only Begotten of the Father: "Jesus knowing that the Father had given all things into his hands, and that he was come from God, and went to God; he riseth from supper" with the intent to wash their feet

(John 13:3–4). Here the scene unfolds. As the One sent from God, Jesus replaced his traditional clothing with a towel draped around him, taking upon him the appearance of a servant and doing a task of the lowliest of servants. The towel that he used was long enough to fasten at the shoulder, wrap around him, and allow excess at the end to use for drying.[2] He began to pour water over the feet of the Apostles to wash them, probably catching the runoff in another container beneath their feet, and then dried them with the towel he wore. Remembering that the men would have been reclining around a *triclinium*, the traditional three-sided table that rested on or near the ground, makes this scene easier to imagine. The men's feet would have been uncovered, with their legs extended behind them as Jesus came by with the water and towel.

One can only imagine the surprise, even shock, that the Apostles experienced with this unprecedented act during the meal. Only Peter, however, is reported to have objected when Jesus approached him. "Lord, dost thou wash my feet?" (John 13:6) or in the Joseph Smith Translation, "Thou needest not to wash my feet." Putting ourselves in the place of Peter, we might understand his discomfort. Certainly, Peter would have gladly washed the feet of Jesus, if requested, but not the other way around. Like Peter, we struggle to believe that Jesus can reach so low. Washing of feet was considered so demeaning that Jewish aristocrats would not assign their Jewish servants to perform the task; only non-Jewish slaves could be so charged.[3]

How, we may ask, can Jesus love and sacrifice for a sinner so proud and rebellious as I am (see *Hymns*, no. 193)? We can readily accept Jesus as our Lord, Master, Redeemer, and

Savior—but not our lowliest servant! So when Jesus responds to Peter, "What I do thou knowest not now; but thou shalt know hereafter," Peter was still confused and again protested, "Thou shalt never wash my feet." Again, the text reminds us that what Jesus is doing is tied to what awaits him "hereafter." The Apostles will not be able to fully appreciate what he is illustrating until after his mortal mission is complete. Giving Peter a greater hint, Jesus warned, "If I wash thee not, thou hast no part with me" (John 13:7–8). Peter must have begun to understand, because at this point, he asked Jesus to not stop with his feet but to wash all of him. I have tried to understand why Peter resisted so long and what Jesus wanted him to see.

In an unrelated and unexpected way, I discovered insight to better appreciate how washing feet in this setting illustrates an aspect of the Atonement of Jesus Christ. During the Christmas season several years ago, I came up with a brilliant idea for a gift for friends who have everything. I decided to give them an experience that would provide a brief moment of pampering and relaxed conversation. Without previous appointment, I visited each of their homes with a variety of nail polishes, buffers, and a foot-soaking basin in hand, and an offer for a Christmas pedicure. Each visit began with complete surprise and guarded appreciation but ended with evidence of a sweet bonding experience. All of this I think I expected. What I didn't expect was the number of my friends who suddenly had a quick emergency in the other room while I was filling the small basin with warm water. It happened often enough that I began to watch for it. Where did they go? What was the sudden emergency? Knowing that every pedicure begins with foot washing, I sensed that they opted to first wash their feet in private before putting them in my basin of sudsy water.

Besides the fact that Peter did not want to humiliate the Savior to the position of slave and foot washer, are there other reasons he may have resisted? Because he knew his feet were dirty, was he hoping to hide the filth from Jesus's view, thinking perhaps Jesus hadn't noticed? Remembering Peter's initial rejection to Jesus's act, "Thou needest not to wash my feet" (Joseph Smith Translation, John 13:6), did Peter think he could easily wash himself without drawing help from or bothering the Master? Seen from this perspective, I wonder if Jesus wasn't reminding Peter and all of us that he knows we are dirty—very dirty—including impure and sullied habits, desires, and attributes that we can easily hide from the world—but not from him. Dust-covered feet reflect the hardships and fatigue of the day and can represent all of our needs, even our humblest ones.

The Savior also knows that as much as we like to think otherwise, we cannot truly cleanse ourselves from the filth of the world and mortality. It is only through the cleansing power of the Atonement that we ever become truly and completely clean. When we recognize and embrace that truth, we will run to turn our filthiness over to the Savior, hiding nothing at all, and ask for his unbounded love to thoroughly wash us. His love for us stretches even to become our servant. That may be hard for us to accept, but the Savior is telling us that we must embrace this view of the condescension of God. Considered from a different angle, while the Twelve partook of the bread and wine of the feast, the Bread of Life and Living Water purified them in ways they could never realize on their own. One biblical scholar interpreted the scene

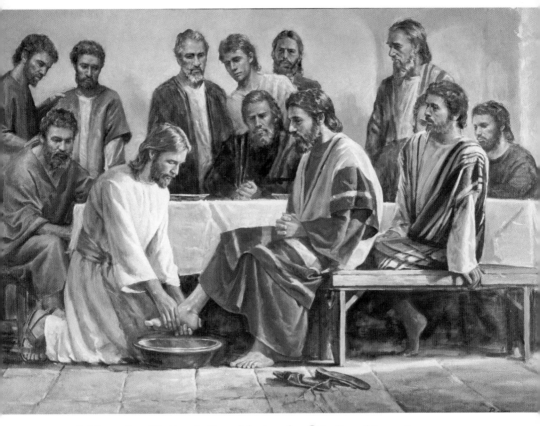

Del Parson, Jesus Washing the Feet of the Apostles. © *Intellectual Reserve, Inc.*

this way: "[Jesus] rises from the settledness of supper and lays aside the protectiveness (and perhaps attractiveness) of clothing. And he washes feet."[4] Like his garments that he laid aside to pour out water to cleanse others, the Savior laid down his life, poured out or emptied himself, and took up his life again—all to save each one of us.

Completing the task of foot washing, Jesus returned to his place at the table and again covered himself in his traditional garments, saying, "Ye call me Master and Lord: and ye say well; for so *I am*" (John 13:13; emphasis added). After his descent to a place of servitude, he ascends to his place as Jehovah, the Great I Am, to teach a second reason for washing their feet in that setting. He explained, "If I then, your Lord and Master, have washed your feet; ye also ought to wash one another's feet. For I have given you an example, that ye should do as I have done to you. Verily, verily, I say unto you, The servant is not greater than his lord; neither he that is sent greater than he that sent him" (John 13:14–16). It isn't enough to be willing and desirous to wash the Savior's feet or even to allow him to wash our feet. We need to be ready to wash each other's feet, to love one another as the Savior loves us, even to humble ourselves to selflessly serve one another, including those who do not yet know and follow the Master. In short, when we love others as Jesus loves, we will recognize the divine in every son and daughter of God and lose ourselves in service to them.

In the synoptic Gospels, Jesus taught, "For whether is greater, he that sitteth at meat, or he that serveth? Is not he that sitteth at meat? but I am among you as he that serveth" (Luke 22:27; see also Matthew 20:26–27). Jesus Christ offers us his boundless love whether he appears as Servant or Master. The Apostle Paul recorded a similar truth to the Philippians, perhaps already known as a poem or canticle that Paul applied to Jesus:

Who being in the form of God,
thought it not robbery to be equal with God:
But made himself of no reputation,
and took upon him the form of a servant,
and was made in the likeness of men:

And being found in fashion as a man,

he humbled himself, and became obedient unto death,

even the death of the cross. (Philippians 2:5–8)

If we will readily and repeatedly accept that Jesus loves us, we will graciously acknowledge our divine indebtedness to him by entrusting him with all our sins and weaknesses, knowing he alone can cleanse us. Then, with our souls filled with the love of Jesus Christ, we will show that same love to others in meek and lowly service. In this way, we invite them to find the Savior's love. "If ye know these things," Jesus summarized, "happy are ye if ye do them" (John 13:17). In other words, happiness comes not by merely knowing and teaching this truth; happiness is the gift we receive when we actively engage in it.

The True Vine

The Savior's sacrifice for us accomplished more than cleansing us from sin and evil. His sacrifice empowers us to produce good fruit—and lots of it. In the first seven verses of John 15, Jesus illustrated how we may remain faithful and fruitful disciples. In this allegory, he identified himself as "the true vine," the Father as the gardener or husbandman, and us as the branches that have life only as we "abide" or remain wholeheartedly committed to Jesus, the only true, real, or authentic support for a fruitful life.

Vine imagery was common in the ancient world, including among the Israelites. Isaiah, Jeremiah, and Ezekiel each described God's covenant people, or Israel, as a potentially fruitful vineyard that repeatedly disappointed the Lord by producing only bitter fruit. The prophets warned that a vine that produces no fruit at all or consistently produces bitter fruit is finally good only for fuel (Isaiah 5:1–7; 27:2–6; Jeremiah 2:21; 12:10–13; Ezekiel 15:1–8; 17:5–10).

One of the most striking embellishments on the temple in Jerusalem was the vine made of pure gold that adorned the entryway into the sanctuary. Josephus, an eyewitness of Herod's magnificent temple, noted the "largeness and fine workmanship" of the golden vine[5] and that the golden clusters that hung on the vine were as tall as a man."[6] In contrast to Israel's failed attempts to produce sustained obedience and loyalty to God, Jesus proclaimed himself as the "true vine," the only sweet-fruit-producing vine. Israel, or God's covenant people, is not the true source of life. Jesus Christ is the only source. In contrast to a golden vine of adornment that can never reproduce, Jesus presented himself as the only way whereby sustained spiritual nourishment multiplies and satisfies forever. In his humble and selfless manner, as the true vine, Jesus then gives all credit and glory to the Gardener, his Father, who oversees and authorizes the entire process of eternal salvation. Considering the sentence that immediately precedes the vine imagery, "Arise, let us go hence," (John 14:31), perhaps Jesus and the Eleven had left the upper room and were walking toward Gethsemane, going past the temple and massive golden vine, when he said, "I am the true vine" (John 15:1).

Jesus explained to the Eleven the consequences for not bearing fruit and the pruning necessary for branches if they will continue to produce good fruit. "Every branch in me that beareth not fruit he taketh away: and every branch that beareth fruit, he purgeth it, that it may bring forth more fruit. Now ye are clean through the word which I have spoken unto you"

(John 15:2–3). The Greek word here, translated "purge," is other places rendered as "cleanse" or "purify," as in morally free from stain, or "moral purity."[7] To be morally free from worldly stains requires us to repent through faith in Christ that he will purify or purge us from the evil. The word has also been considered to mean "prop up."[8] No matter how low we fall, through faith and repentance in his name, he will lift us up and make us fruitful again. Finally, these verses indicate that purging, propping up, and purifying are supported by spiritual nourishment received through hearing and heeding his spoken "word."

A vinedresser follows a two-step process in pruning to encourage more fruit. In the winter, he cuts off and removes dry and withered branches, and when the vine spouts new leaves in the spring, he "purges" or pinches off smaller shoots from the fruit-bearing branches to concentrate nourishment on the good branches to produce even more fruit.[9] To bear good fruit, we must be filled with more and more of his love and develop a deeper desire to follow his teachings. Jesus is the embodiment of all that he teaches. When he lives in us, his words are "written not with ink, but with the Spirit of the living God; not in tables of stone, but in fleshy tables of the heart" (2 Corinthians 3:3). When we obey his commandments because we love him, we become seamless extensions of him. When his word lives in us, the entire plant—stalk and branches—together becomes the true vine without any evidence to distinguish where one part ends and the other begins.

Elias Chacour, a Palestinian Christian who lives near Galilee, wrote of the resulting phenomenon when various grafts are introduced in fig trees to explain how Jews and Palestinians, whether natural or grafted branches, soon merge together into God's chosen people of faith. He described that his "father had grafted six different kinds of fig trees together to make a delightful new tree. Beneath the rough bark where my hand rested, I knew that the living wood had fused together so perfectly that, should I cut the tree down, I could never see where one variety stopped and the other began."[10] The imagery of bonding branches in vines and fig trees echoes the Apostle Paul's depiction of the Church as various parts of one body—but that body to which we all may belong is the body of Christ (see 1 Corinthians 12:12–27).

Several years ago, I read a little booklet written by a Christian pastor who reported an exchange with an owner of a large vineyard in Northern California. The vineyard owner related his insights to this scriptural passage after years of working in the fields. "New branches have a natural tendency to trail down and grow along the ground," the vineyard owner explained, "but they don't bear fruit down there. When branches grow along the ground, the leaves get coated in dust. When it rains, they get muddy and mildewed. The branch becomes sick and useless." To which the pastor asked, "What do you do? Cut it off and throw it away?" The vineyard owner quickly answered, "Oh, no! The branch is much too valuable for that. We go through the vineyard with a bucket of water looking for those branches. We lift them up and wash them off. . . . Then we wrap them around the trellis or tie them up. Pretty soon they're thriving."[11]

The vineyard owner's experience of washing sullied branches echoes the Old Testament prophet Jeremiah's portrayal of God's people as a potentially fruitful vineyard that too often produced bitter fruit, even after being washed with

cleansing agents and "much soap" (Jeremiah 2:21–22; see also Isaiah 5:1–7). As inheritors of fallen earth, we have a tendency to bend downwards toward the course of least resistance, where we are easily tainted by the world and lose the love of God in us. Through repentance and the Lord's cleansing forgiveness, we may again be propped up, nourished, and purified and return to becoming fruitful.

Jesus used the word *abide* seven times in four verses to describe the necessary relationship between fruitful branches and the vine.

> **Abide** in me, and I in you. As the branch cannot bear fruit of itself, except it **abide** in the vine; no more can ye, except ye **abide** in me.
>
> I am the vine, ye are the branches: He that **abideth** in me, and I in him, the same bringeth forth much fruit: for without me ye can do nothing.
>
> If a man **abide** not in me, he is cast forth as a branch, and is withered; and men gather them, and cast them into the fire, and they are burned. If ye **abide** in me, and my word **abide** in you, ye shall ask what ye will, and it shall be done unto you." (John 15:4–7; emphasis added).

The imagery intensifies the meaning of abide to suggest far more than simply remaining loyal or connected. Abiding with him means that disciples will stand steadfast to his teachings, even when persecution, questions, temptations, or tragedy try to pull them down. Abiding with him means that disciples desire to serve him everlastingly more than they desire the praise of the world. The result for the vine and branches is vibrant, mutual in-dwelling that produces the very fullness of joy for everyone. He explained his desired outcome to the Eleven, saying, "These things have I spoken unto you, that my joy might remain in you, and that your joy might be full" (John 15:11).

In the October 2016 general conference, Elder D. Todd Christofferson explored the rich relationship that results when we abide in the Savior and he abides in us.

> To "continue in" or "abide in" the Savior's love means to receive His grace and be perfected by it. To receive His grace, we must have faith in Jesus Christ and keep His commandments, including repenting of our sins, being baptized for the remission of sins, receiving the Holy Ghost, and continuing in the path of obedience. God will always love us, but He cannot save us in our sins. . . .
>
> Beyond rendering the penitent person guiltless and spotless . . . there is a second vital aspect of abiding in the love of God. Abiding in His love will enable us to realize our full potential, to become even as He is. . . .
>
> To abide in God's love in this sense means to submit fully to His will. It means to accept His correction when needed, "for whom the Lord loveth he chasteneth" (Heb. 12:6). It means to love and serve one another as Jesus has loved and served us (John 15:12). It means to learn "to abide the law of a celestial kingdom" so that we can "abide a celestial glory" (D&C 88:22). For Him to be able to make of us what we can become, our Heavenly Father pleads with us to yield "to the enticings of the Holy Spirit, and [put] off the natural man and [become] a saint through the atonement of Christ the Lord, and [become] as a child, submissive, meek, humble,

patient, full of love, willing to submit to all things which the Lord seeth fit to inflict upon him, even as a child doth submit to his father" (Mosiah 3:19).[12]

Fruit is the desired outcome in the allegory. God's greatest redemptive purpose is to produce fruit. He has invited us to participate in this glorious process of fruit bearing or transformation. "I am the vine, ye are the branches," he stated. Only by abiding in Jehovah, the Great *I Am*—the Always Existing One—and the Great I Am dwelling in us can we become like he is. Only as extensions of the true vine do we fully internalize his word, produce Christlike character and attributes, and thereby reach all of God's children to invite them to learn of him and taste the sweetness of his word. Without his strength, we will wither and die. With his life-giving power, we can do and become all that he created us to do and be. As the Apostle Paul testified, "I can do all things through Christ which strengtheneth me" (Philippians 4:13).

The Great Intercessory Prayer

Having completed his teaching of the Eleven in the upper room, either still in the room or at Gethsemane, Jesus "lifted his eyes to heaven" to pray to the Father for them and for all those who would receive them. In part, the Savior petitioned the Father as follows:

> And now come I to thee; and these things I speak in the world, that they might have my joy fulfilled in themselves. . . .
>
> I pray not that thou shouldest take them out of the world, but that thou shouldest keep them from the evil. . . .

Harry Anderson, Jesus Christ. © *Intellectual Reserve, Inc.*

Neither pray I for these alone, but for them also which shall believe on me through their words;

That they all may be one; as thou, Father, art in me, and
I in thee, that they also may be one in us: that the world may
believe that thou hast sent me . . .

That the love wherewith thou hast loved me may be in
them, and I in them. (John 17:13, 15, 20–21, 26)

In what must be among the most selfless and poignant
prayers ever uttered, Jesus imagines something akin to a
chain of perfect love that forms a complete circle or an eternal round.[13] Through the perfect love of God, the Father is
gloriously united with the Son who did all that the Father
asked him to do (John 17:4). Next, because of the Savior's
sacrifice of selfless love, we may be resplendently united with
the Son as his covenant sons and daughters. This empowering
and fruitful unity occurs when we (1) willingly turn over our
filthiness to him, trusting that he alone can cleanse us and
(2) steadfastly abide in him to bear the fruit of joy that comes
from obedience to his commandments and to represent
him throughout the world. Finally, because of the great and
infinite Atonement of Jesus Christ, we may become begotten sons and daughters of God and joint-heirs with Christ
(see Romans 8:14–17, John 1:12, and D&C 76:24). Through
the power of Christ's matchless love and willing acceptance
as manifest through repentance and obedience, we are again
reconciled to the Father with transformed characters, desires,
and capacity to love one another as Jesus loves them.

Jesus taught that if we would come closer to him, we need
to change our relationship with the world without departing
out of the world. By separating our desires from what the
world glorifies, even when surrounded by greed, deceit, and

vengeance, we welcome the tutoring that uniquely comes through the Holy Spirit. Grace by grace, our hearts and minds are gradually transformed to be like that of our Savior's because we have allowed him to be in us as the Father is in him. In a holy familial reunion, we become "one" with the Father and his Son, even sealed to them as family forever.

On the eve before his crucifixion and shortly before his suffering in Gethsemane, fully aware that his "hour had come," Jesus orchestrated events in an upper room to teach his disciples the transformative power of perfect love. He told them, "Greater love hath no man than this, that he lay down his life for his friends" (John 15:13). The fact that "while we were yet sinners, Christ died for us" makes the power of such love all the more transcendent (Romans 5:8). He has given each of us the invitation to abide by his "new commandment . . . that ye love one another; as I have loved you. . . . By this shall all men know that ye are my disciples, if ye have love one to another" (John 13:34–35). This Easter season, let us pray for greater faith to embrace the love he offers us and in turn, multiply his love by the way we respect and serve one another.

Notes

1. Even though verse 2 in the KJV reports that the dinner had ended (see John 13:2), one can see that they were still eating in verse 26. More accurately, verse 2 would read "supper being served," the translation suggested by Frank F. Judd Jr., *The Essential New Testament Companion: Key Insights to Your Gospel Study* (American Fork, UT: Covenant Communications, 2014), 47; or "and supper was now in process," the translation suggested by F. F. Bruce, *The Gospel According to John* (Grand Rapids, MI: Eerdmans, 1983), 279.

2. Andreas J. Köstenberger, *John: Baker Exegetical Commentary on the New Testament* (Grand Rapids, MI: Baker Academic, 2004), 404.

3. Rabbi Joshua B. Levi taught, "All manner of service that a slave must render to his master a student must render to his teacher, except that of taking off his shoe"; the associated note adds: "Only a Canaanite slave performs this menial service, and a student performing it might be mistaken for such a slave," *b.Ketub.* 96a.

4. Thomas L. Brodie, *The Gospel According to John: A Literary and Theological Commentary* (New York: Oxford University Press, 1993), 447.

5. Josephus, *Antiquities*, 15.11.3.

6. Josephus, *Wars*, 5.5.4. In latter Rabbinic literature, priests hung free-will offerings on the golden vine in the form of a gold-shaped "leaf, or a berry, or a cluster" until the "Temple treasury was in need" and the "treasurer took from the vine as much as was required" (*Middoth* 3.8). See also Tacitus, *History* 5.5, for the Roman historian's notation of this breathtaking golden vine.

7. *Theological Dictionary of the New Testament*, 10 vols. (Grand Rapids, MI: Eerdmans, 1965), 3:414.

8. Köstenberger, *John*, 451.

9. Raymond E. Brown, *The Gospel According to John XIII–XXI* (New York: Doubleday, 1970), 675.

10. Elias Chacour, *Blood Brothers* (Grand Rapids, MI: Chosen Books, 1984), 137.

11. Bruce Wilkinson, *Secrets of the Vine* (Sister, OR: Multnomah, 2001), 34–35.

12. D. Todd Christofferson, "Abide in My Love," *Ensign*, November 2016, 48–49.

13. For the basis of this imagery, see Köstenberger, *John*, 457.

MOURNING WITH HOPE

Hank R. Smith

Hank R. Smith is an assistant professor of
ancient scripture at Brigham Young University.

On the spring morning of Sunday, 20 March 1842, Joseph Smith stood in a grove of trees near the construction site of the Nauvoo Temple. He was speaking to a group of Saints who had gathered to hear him preach on baptism. However, because of the recent death of a young child, a two-year-old girl named Marian S. Lyon, the Prophet had altered his remarks to include thoughts on death and resurrection. At one point in his sermon, the Prophet said, "[We] mourn the loss but we do not mourn as those without hope."[1]

Joseph's statement may be taken to mean that in The Church of Jesus Christ of Latter-day Saints we do mourn the deaths of our beloved friends and family members, but we mourn differently than others. One might say we mourn with hope. Where does the hope that Joseph spoke of stem from? The answer to this question is significant. Death is both universal and personal—perhaps more than any other experience of mortal life. All of God's children must deal with deep loss throughout mortal life, and all must eventually contemplate their own assured death.

The Sting of Death

Each individual has experienced or will experience the aching and sometimes overwhelming grief that comes with the passing of a cherished individual. Our Heavenly Father has given each of us a remarkable mind. With concentration, we can recall in our minds the voices and the laughter of those we love who have died. The human mind's ability to draw on memories from even decades ago is astounding. In our mind's eye, many can still recall a smile of a love one now passed on or a familiar phrase they would often repeat. Despite the time that has gone by, in a still moment we may hear the voice of a cherished family member or friend echoing across our memories, often with incredible clarity—a voice of a person whom we long to see again, to talk to again, to laugh with again. In such moments we feel both sweet happiness and piercing heartache. These experiences bring to mind the scriptural phrase, "The sting of death"[2]—the deep and inescapable pain of missing terribly a beloved mother or father, grandmother or grandfather, sister or brother, aunt or uncle, a close friend, or perhaps most painful of all, a child.

Jacob, the fifth son of Lehi, described death and hell as a monster.[3] With this unique description, Jacob may teach us, at least in part, why human beings are naturally afraid of death. The word "monster" might take us back to our childhood bedrooms.

"The sting of death" may refer to the deep and inseperable pain of missing a loved one.

How is death like the monsters of a dark closet or the dreaded monsters we were sure were lurking under our bed? What is it that children actually fear? Perhaps our fear of a monster was actually a fear of the unknown. Without knowing what the monster actually looked like, our young imagination was free to create the most hideous and fearsome creature it could devise. We knew the monster was both powerful and merciless. We knew that no matter how we struggled to fight or how sincerely we cried out for sympathy, the monster could not be stopped and would not choose to stop until we were destroyed.

Perhaps Jacob used this description because death may seem both unknown and merciless. The fear of death is natural to our human experience and it, amid other reasons, keeps us striving to stay alive as long as possible. Like children, we feel vulnerable in the face of the unknown, the powerful, and the merciless. Epicurus, the ancient Greek philosopher wrote, "Against all other hazards it is possible for us to gain security for ourselves but so far as death is concerned all of us human beings inhabit a city without walls."[4] In other words, death brings a sense of vulnerability unmatched by any other fact of life. We stand in its path, completely exposed and without any form of defense.

When we experience the passing of a loved one, we may, in the grip of inescapable grief, even cry out in anguish or anger against the monster of death and hell. Said Ralph Waldo Emerson, "Sorrow makes us all children again—destroys all differences of intellect. The wisest know nothing."[5] The monster seems to steal our cherished loved ones without remorse. The following comments found on an online forum for those mourning a death may give us a glimpse of the experience:

> There are no words and not enough tears to reflect the immensity of our loss. Everything is changed. A [thief] has robbed me of my future. The space she inhabited in our lives has become a void where her laughter and light no longer lives, where questions remain unanswered.[6]

> The first few days were a surreal nightmare—I actually asked people to wake me up. Then I just started putting one foot in front of the other and walking through all the logistics of a death and learning to be alone. . . . I live in a wide awake

coma. I'm here walking, talking, writing but not really here at all. All the meaning of life was drained from me in that one horrible moment.[7]

It has been over a decade for me now. . . . She is fixed in time, she never grew older the way I have. She remains the vital woman she was before the cancer in my memory. But even now, something will make me think of something about her and first I smile and get happy and then I get really sad. You remember the blessings and then you remember the loss. It still hurts.[8]

I cannot describe how the loss affects you physically, emotionally, spiritually—every way possible. I only know that it did—and my whole body ached with sorrow. I didn't think it was possible to cry that much, but I did. I didn't think it was possible to be so sad and miss someone so much, but I did.[9]

My husband of almost 20 years died suddenly 2 1/2 years ago. I was numb at first, but the devastation set in very quickly. Half of me disappeared. I felt empty, lost, disoriented, and totally depressed. I only need the simplest reminder of Sam and I start tearing up. He was my best friend first, then my love.[10]

Dealing with Death

Cultures and individuals across the globe seek to cope with this knowledge and mitigate the pain in unique ways. The "sting of death" is no respecter of persons. Said Roman poet Horace,

"Death with impartial step knocks at the huts of the poor and at the palace of kings."[11] All humanity will experience death—either as an observer and participant. Sorrow, fear, and despair are the common response, especially to those without the knowledge of the plan of salvation. Modern philosopher and Cambridge professor Stephen Cave has said, "We have to live in the knowledge that the worst thing that can possibly happen one day surely will, the end of all our projects, our hopes, our dreams, of our individual world. We each live in the shadow of a personal apocalypse. And that's frightening. It's terrifying."[12] British novelist Howard Jacobson wrote, "How do you go on knowing that you will never again—not ever, ever—see the person you have loved? How do you survive a single hour, a single minute, a single second of that knowledge? How do you hold yourself together?"[13] Ancient Greek playwright Euripides wrote to a loved one who had passed away, "Come back! Even as a shadow, / even as a dream."[14]

There are some who seek to avoid death entirely. They hope to sidestep the sting and search for a way to escape the grasp of the monster. Corporate executive Larry Ellison is on record declaring his desire to live forever and has donated more than 430 million dollars to anti-aging research. "Death has never made any sense to me," he told his biographer, Mike Wilson. "How can a person be there and then just vanish, just not be there?" Larry Page, another corporate executive, has made the biggest bet on longevity yet, founding California Life Company, an antiaging research center, with an investment of up to 750 million dollars. Despite the fortunes that have been poured into the fight against death, none have proven to be very effective.[15] This reality caused author Susan Jacoby to write, "Acceptance of the point at which intelligence and its inventions can no longer battle the ultimate natural master, death, is a true affirmation of what it means to be human."[16]

Some take a lighthearted approach. Billy Standley of Mechanicsburg, Ohio, purchased three burial plots so he could be buried in a large casket allowing his body to sit atop his 1967 Harley Davidson.[17] George Swanson of Hempfield County, Pennsylvania, purchased twelve burial plots so he could be buried in the driver's seat of his 1984 white Corvette (which only had 27,000 miles on the odometer).[18] The family of Pittsburgh Steelers fan James Smith transformed the funeral home with a small stage and furniture from Smith's living room. The deceased was placed in his favorite recliner, remote control in hand, so he could comfortably watch a loop of Steelers football on TV.[19] When Judy Sunday passed away in 2013, her family and friends held a memorial at her favorite bowling alley, where they spelled "RIP Judy" in pins and then knocked them down with the dolly-mounted casket.[20]

Humor can be a coping mechanism for those dealing with death. Actor Woody Allen is said to have remarked, "I'm not afraid to die, I just don't want to be there when it happens." Eighty-eight-year-old prankster Chet Finch of Oregon had his barber mail handwritten cards to friends two months after Chet's death with heaven as the return address.[21] British prime minister Winston Churchill is said to have remarked, "I am prepared to meet my Maker. Whether my Maker is prepared for the great ordeal of meeting me is another matter."[22] Legend holds that on his deathbed, Oscar Wilde is reported to have said, "Either that wallpaper goes or I do." Some believe that he actually said, "This wallpaper and I are fighting a duel to the death.

All humanity will have to deal with death on their mortal journey—
either as an observer or as a participant.

Either it goes or I do."[23] Bertrand Russell once quipped, "We are all like the turkey who wakes up [Thanksgiving] morning expecting lunch as usual. Things can go wrong at any time."[24]

Different cultures have passed down ancient death traditions for thousands of years. Famadihana is a funerary tradition of the Malagasy people in Madagascar. The Malagasy, in what is termed "the turning of the bones," bring forth the bodies of their ancestors from the family tombs and rewrap them in fresh cloth, then dance with the corpses around the tomb to live music. This tradition is akin to Memorial Day in the US, a time for the Malagasy people to remember their dead relatives and loved ones.

For Torajans on the Indonesian island of Sulawesi, the death of the family member isn't an abrupt, final, severing event like it is in the West. Instead, death is just one step in a long, gradually unfolding process. The bodies of deceased loved ones are tended to in the home; they are dressed, offered food, and are even part of family pictures for weeks, months, or even years after death.

The majority of human beings deal with death in a much more traditional way. Many turn to mourning in private. These can be the darkest and most difficult times of life. After returning to her home the night of the funeral for her husband who was killed in an accident in the streets of Paris, the famed scientist Madame Marie Curie wrote this entry in her diary: "They filled the grave and put sheaves of flowers on it. Everything is over. Pierre is sleeping his last sleep beneath the earth; it is the end of everything, everything, everything."[25]

Latter-day Saints are not immune to the tragedy of death. The faithful are not exempt from grief. Try to imagine the heartache of Stillman Pond, who with his wife Maria, joined the Church in 1841. The Ponds had been among the first group to flee Nauvoo in February of 1846. Later that year, in Winter Quarters, Nebraska, the Saints were ravaged by malaria, cholera, and consumption. It was there where Stillman Pond buried nine of his eleven children and his sweet wife, Maria. Historian Richard E. Bennett estimated that a minimum of 723 Latter-day Saint pioneers died between June 1846 and May 1847 in settlements on both sides of the Missouri River and back along the Iowa trail. Nearly half the deaths were infants two years old and younger.[26] (Comparatively, approximately 250–70 handcart pioneers died in the Willie and Martin companies in 1856.)[27] Words cannot express the heartbreak Stillman Pond and those like him experienced. In *Macbeth*, Shakespeare wrote, "Give sorrow words. The grief that does not speak whispers the o'erfraught heart and bids it break."[28]

The painful reality of mourning is also not foreign to prophets and apostles. All men and women, including the Lord's anointed servants, must wrestle with the pain of death. Job asked, "If a man die, shall he live again?"[29] The Lord has said, "Thou shalt weep for the loss of them that die" (D&C 42:45). President Gordon B. Hinckley, who lost his beloved wife, Marjorie, after sixty-seven years of marriage, said the following:

> When the last of life's breath is drawn, there is a finality comparable to no other finality. When a father and mother lay the remains of a beloved child in the cold of the grave, there is grief almost inconsolable. When a husband buries the companion of his life, there is a loneliness that is poignant and unrelieved. When a wife closes the casket on the remains of her beloved husband, there are wounds that seem never to heal. When children are bereft of parents who loved and nurtured them, there is an abject destitution comparable to none other. Life is sacred, and death is somber. Life is buoyant and hopeful. Death is solemn and dark. It is awesome in its silence and certainty.[30]

A testimony does not exempt anyone from the deep sense of loss that accompanies death.

Speaking of the loss of one of his wives, Sarah, whose death was followed shortly by one of his daughters, Zina, President Joseph F. Smith said, "I cannot yet dwell on the scenes of the recent past. Our hearts have been tried to the core. Not that the end of mortal life has come to two of the dearest souls on earth to me, so much as at the sufferings of our loved ones, which we were utterly powerless to relieve. Oh! How helpless is mortal man in the face of sickness unto death!"[31] In his first general conference address following Marjorie's death, President Hinckley remarked, "Before I married her, she had been the girl of my dreams, to use the words of a song then popular. She was my dear companion for more than two-thirds of a century, my equal before the Lord, really my superior. And now in my old age, she has again become the girl of my dreams."[32]

Recent Apostles such as Richard G. Scott, L. Tom Perry, Dallin H. Oaks, and Russell M. Nelson have buried a spouse during their lives. Speaking of the passing of his wife, Dantzel, President Nelson recounted the following experience:

> While I was at home on a rare Saturday with no assignment, we had worked together. She had washed our clothing. I had helped to carry it, fold it, and put it in place. Then while we were sitting on the sofa, holding hands, enjoying a program on television, my precious Dantzel slipped peacefully into eternity. Her passing came suddenly and unexpectedly. Just four days earlier, our doctor's report at a routine checkup indicated that her laboratory tests were good. After my efforts to revive her proved fruitless, feelings of shock and sorrow overwhelmed me. My closest friend, angel mother

of our 10 children, grandmother of our 56 grandchildren, had been taken.[33]

Stories like these tug on our heartstrings because we all will experience (or we are conscious of the reality that we some-day will experience) scenes like them.

Without hope, death's finality is crushing. This monster's power is devastating. Its sting is piercing and agonizing. The light and energy of life are gone, and a heavy and complete darkness closes in until the bereaved is entirely overcome, engulfed in impenetrable grief.

Light, Life, and Hope

When the people of the Book of Mormon were encompassed in the overwhelming darkness described in 3 Nephi 8, the record states that they were "mourning and howling and weeping" (3 Nephi 8:21). Sometime toward the end of the three days of complete darkness, they heard a voice. Amid the message given to them they heard, "I am Jesus Christ the Son of God. . . . I am the light and the life of the world."[34] Not long after the voice had spoken, "the darkness dispersed from off the face of the land . . . and the mourning, and the weep-ing, and the wailing. . . . did cease; and their mourning was turned into joy, and their lamentations into the praise and thanksgiving unto the Lord Jesus Christ, their Redeemer."[35]

Not long after, the resurrected Lord appeared to the Nephite people. Their confusion about what was happening slowly turned into comprehension. As they processed the real-ity of his presence, and all that it meant, they fell to the earth

Arnold Friberg. Christ Appearing in the Western Hemisphere.

in worship. This was not a dream. This was not a hallucination. It was Jesus Christ. He was right there in front of them to see, hear, and touch. It was overwhelming in every sense. Among many other things, his presence was an irrefutable witness of life after death—his life after death and the life after death of so many loved ones. Annihilation quickly became a myth of yesterday. After this day, all about yesterday would seem like a completely different life. It is no wonder why Elder Jeffrey R. Holland referred to it as "the day of days!"[36]

The Lord Jesus Christ, our Savior and Redeemer, our brother and friend, turns darkness into light and mourning into joy. His entire existence witnesses the reality that death is not the end. Like the first glimmer of dawn turns into a glorious morning sun after the darkest and coldest of nights, he has gloriously risen as the supreme embodiment of light and life. Weeping did endure for a night, but joy has come with the rising Son.

Without the slightest equivocation, Latter-day Saints declare the reality of historical Christianity. We declare, "Christ actually lived, died, and was resurrected and that the glad tidings of His Resurrection spawned a movement and a doctrine that continue to change lives. If there is one recurring theological constancy of the Book of Mormon, it is that Christ was born, that He lived and died in Jerusalem, that He was literally resurrected, and that His atoning sacrifice for sin happened in time and place."[37] G. Stanley Hall, an American psychologist, wrote in 1915, "The most essential claim of Christianity is to have removed the fear of death and made the king of terrors into a good friend and boon companion."[38]

The Resurrection of Jesus Christ is the very core of who we are as a Church and who we are as disciples of Christ. Joseph Smith declared, "The fundamental principles of our religion are the testimony of the Apostles and Prophets, concerning Jesus

Christ, that He died, was buried, and rose again the third day, and ascended into heaven; and all other things which pertain to our religion are only appendages to it."[39] Latter-day Saints boldly believe in literal everlasting life. We do not fear an unending consciousness. Said President Dieter F. Uchtdorf, "In light of what we know about our eternal destiny, is it any wonder that whenever we face the bitter endings of life, they seem unacceptable to us? There seems to be something inside of us that resists endings. Why is this? Because we are made of the stuff of eternity. We are eternal beings, children of the Almighty God, whose name is Endless and who promises eternal blessings without number. Endings are not our destiny."[40]

In the Bible Dictionary we read, "Christianity is founded on the greatest of all miracles, the Resurrection of our Lord. If that be admitted, other miracles cease to be improbable."[41] In other words, if Jesus Christ was really resurrected, if he really does now live forever as a glorified being, what else can he do? What else will he do? Certainly, having a teenage farmboy translate the Book of Mormon and restore his (Christ's) Church does not fall outside the expertise of one who has power over life and death. Such an orchestration would seem simple for such a being. In fact, using *unlikely* scenarios may be the preferred method to a being whose Resurrection was an achievement which had never been accomplished before in the history of the world. Wrote scientist Henry Eyring, "The Creator of the universe almost certainly knows enough about how things work to control and manipulate event to meet his purposes. . . . Revelations and miracles seem like the natural consequences of having a compassionate and just Creator of the universe interested in human events."[42]

Grant Romney Clawson, Jesus Appearing to the Five Hundred.
© *Intellectual Reserve, Inc.*

The reality of the Resurrection of Jesus Christ has been and continues to be witnessed by many. Among the first to see the resurrected Lord was the chief Apostle Peter, who wrote, "We have not followed cunningly devised fables . . . but were eyewitnesses of his majesty."[43] Elder James E. Talmage referred to Christ's Resurrection as "the greatest miracle and the most glorious fact of history . . . and is attested by evidence more conclusive than that which rests our acceptance of historical events in general."[44] Mary Magdalene, Cleophas, Peter, James, John, Thomas, Paul, Joseph Smith, Lorenzo Snow, and many others, both ancient and modern, have witnessed that they have seen him and have heard his voice.

The text of the New Testament reveals Jesus's followers gaining, not losing, confidence following his death. This is explained best by a powerful belief in his Resurrection. In promoting the gospel message, the ancient Apostles appealed, even when encountering their most ruthless opponents, to seemingly common knowledge concerning the reality of the Resurrection. Peter and John and the others of Christ's followers did not leave the area to declare that Christ was raised from the dead. Rather, they went right back to the city of Jerusalem, where, if what they were teaching was false, the deceptiveness would be most blatantly evident. The Pharisee Gamaliel suggested that what Peter and John preached may "be of God."[45] Why would he do such a thing if he had any compelling evidence that their message was spurious? Concerning the value of the testimonies of Matthew, Mark, Luke, and John, F. F. Bruce, Rylands Professor of Biblical Criticism at the University of Manchester, says, "Had there been any tendency to depart from the facts in any material respect, the possible presence of hostile witnesses in the audience would have served as a further corrective."[46]

There are those who say the record of the New Testament cannot be trusted. Archaeological discoveries have bolstered the veracity of the New Testament manuscripts. Because of its unlikely claims, the Bible is held to a higher standard. Said Christian scholar F. F. Bruce, "If the New Testament were a collection of secular writings, their authenticity would generally be regarded as beyond all doubt."[47]

Of course there will be those who insist that Jesus Christ's Resurrection is simply foolish in the enlightened world. They disregard the idea of such a miracle and the notion that miracles exist at all. Renowned intellectual E. F. Schumacher wrote, "The modern world seems to be skeptical about everything that makes demands on man's higher faculties. But it is not at all skeptical about skepticism, which demands hardly anything."[48] Instead, these enlightened skeptics sometimes seek to replace the Christian God with godless science. In writing about what he called the belief "that living beings suddenly made their appearance by pure chance," Schumacher wrote sarcastically, "One can just see it, can't one: organic compounds getting together and surrounding themselves by membranes—nothing could be simpler for these clever compounds—and lo! there is the cell, and once the cell has been born there is nothing to stop the emergence of Shakespeare, although it will obviously take a bit of time. There is therefore no need to speak of miracles."[49]

Now, that isn't to say that we as a church do not appreciate scientific discovery, particularly the theory of evolution. Our gospel is a search for truth, no matter where it is found. However, most Latter-day Saints would probably agree with Dr. Henry Eyring when he wrote, "The [theory] has to include the notion that the dice have been loaded from the beginning in favor of more complex life forms. That is, without intelligent design of the natural laws in such a way as to favor evolution from lower forms to higher forms of life, I don't think the theory holds water."[50] Within a broader perspective produced by acknowledging the omniscience of God, our significant scientific discoveries can be put in their proper place and can be incredibly useful. Elder Russell M. Nelson modeled this when he taught, "Yes, compounds derived from dust—elements of the earth—are combined to make each living cell in our bodies. The miracle of the Resurrection, wondrous as it will be, is marvelously matched by the miracle of our creation in the first place."[51] The methods of science can teach us many things, but they should not be misused to tear down faith—they were never designed to do so.

Despite what critics may say, the fact remains that with His Resurrection, Jesus Christ has driven back and conquered the monster of death. Christ has healed the sting of death and has allowed courage and strength to fill the human heart. Followers of Christ witness as the prophet Abinadi testified when he faced his own impending death. After being falsely accused and condemned to death, Abinadi turned to his captors and affirmed, "There is a resurrection, therefore the grave hath no victory, and the sting of death is swallowed up in Christ. He is the light and the life of the world; yea, a light that is endless, that can never be darkened; yea, and also a life that is endless, that there can be no more death."[52] When one is focused on the Savior and his Resurrection, confidence replaces darkness; hope replaces fear.

In 1842, Eliza R. Snow penned the following poem in which she addressed death itself:

> The darkness that encompass'd thee, is gone;
> There is no frightfulness about thee no . . .
> Since the glorious light
> Of revelation shone upon thy path
> Thou seem'st no more a hideous monster, arm'd
> With as thou art, by inspiration's light,
> Thou hast no look the righteous need to fear.[53]

Easter

Each spring, the Lord teaches us that life and warmth follow the fall and the winter. The "fortunate fall"[54] of man brought about spiritual and physical death. These deaths, crucial to the Lord's plan of salvation, were meant to be overcome. With the budding of the trees and flowers, God teaches us each year that life overpowers death, warmth replaces cold, and light banishes darkness. Martin Luther is credited with saying, "Our Lord has written the promise of the resurrection, not in books alone, but in every leaf in spring-time."[55]

If grading by the significance of what is being celebrated, Easter could be (perhaps should be) thought of as the most important of all the modern holidays. The Resurrection is the "greatest of all events in the history of mankind." President Dieter F. Uchtdorf wrote, "On Easter Sunday we celebrate the most long-awaited and glorious event in the history of the world. It is the day that changed everything. On that day, my life changed. Your life changed. The destiny of all God's children changed. When I think of what the Savior did for us . . . that first Easter Sunday, I want to lift up my voice and shout praises to the Most High God and His Son, Jesus Christ! The gates of heaven are unlocked! The windows of heaven are opened!"[56] For believers, the Easter holiday is a personal recognition of devotion to a literally resurrected Lord.

The scriptures are rife in the reassurance that not only did Christ rise from the dead but all mankind will follow Him through their individual resurrection. Wrote Phillips Brooks, "Let every man and woman count himself immortal. Let him catch the revelation of Jesus in his resurrection. Let him say not merely, 'Christ is risen,' but 'I shall rise.'"[57] The promise is sure. Without any doubt, without any uncertainty, Christ's followers declare each individual will see, hear, talk with, laugh with, and embrace their cherished loved ones again. Their kind mother, their gentle father, their grandparents, their siblings, their best of friends—all will live again. Is there any more important message in all the world?

While we do not know what difficulty the Savior had to endure to ensure resurrection for all mankind, we can assume it was not done with ease. Each time the sting of death is used in the Book of Mormon, it is followed by the word "swallowed."[58] Mormon states simply that the "sting of death" is "swallowed up." Abinadi comments that the "sting of death is swallowed up in Christ." Aaron teaches King Lamoni's father that the "sting of death should be swallowed up in the hopes of his glory." The word "swallow" is often thought of encompassing, covering, or completely surrounding something. In that regard, the knowledge of Christ's Resurrection does swallow up and balm the sting of death. However, the Savior has also repeatedly told us that He has drunk out of "the bitter cup." With such a picture in mind, the sting of death being swallowed up in Christ takes on a different meaning. It was in Christ's partaking of the bitter cup that death was swallowed up and overcome.

Merciful Hope

The certainty of the Resurrection is the only force able to mitigate the shock and bereavement of losing a beloved family member or friend to death. No matter where we "search for peace," every other source will "cease to make [us] whole."[59]

While the deep pain of loss and trauma of a changed daily life is not taken away, the surety of the Resurrection of Jesus Christ can calm the stormy seas of the heart. We are bereaved, but such grief is, mercifully, only temporary. Because of Jesus Christ, "even the darkest night will end and the sun will rise."[60] Our knowledge of the plan of salvation, the Fall of man, the role of death, and the Atonement of Jesus Christ enable us to mourn with hope.

In the April 2009 general conference, President Thomas S. Monson related the story of a member of the Church who was saved, both physically and spiritually, by her knowledge of a certain Resurrection. She and her family lived in East Prussia, but her husband was killed in World War II. She was left alone to care for their four children, the oldest being only seven. While fleeing Prussia for West Germany, a journey of over one thousand miles, she and her children were forced to gather food from fields and forests along the way. As they continued, the weather turned freezing. Without the necessary supplies, she and the children had little protection. One by one, this faithful sister lost each of her children to death—at times digging their graves with a spoon. Her grief was overwhelming and she contemplated ending her own life. President Monson continued:

And then, as these thoughts assailed her, something within her said, "Get down on your knees and pray." She ignored the prompting until she could resist it no longer. She knelt and prayed more fervently than she had in her entire life: "Dear Heavenly Father, I do not know how I can go on. I have nothing left—except my faith in Thee. I feel, Father, amidst the desolation of my soul, an overwhelming gratitude for the atoning sacrifice of Thy Son, Jesus Christ. I cannot express

adequately my love for Him. I know that because He suffered and died, I shall live again with my family; that because
He broke the chains of death, I shall see my children again
and will have the joy of raising them. Though I do not at this
moment wish to live, I will do so, that we may be reunited as
a family and return—together—to Thee."

The woman eventually reached Germany, starving and
emaciated. Shortly thereafter, she bore testimony in a Church
meeting. She stated "that of all the ailing people in her sad-
dened land, she was one of the happiest because she knew
that God lived, that Jesus is the Christ, and that He died and
was resurrected so that we might live again. She testified that
she knew if she continued faithful and true to the end, she
would be reunited with those she had lost and would be saved
in the celestial kingdom of God."[61]

Among other hopeful doctrines, the woman must have
been bolstered by the knowledge that her children and husband we together in the spirit world. They were now in the
company of many family members, ancestors who had passed
on before them. President Nelson once remarked, "Our limited perspective would be enlarged if we could witness the
reunion on the other side of the veil, when doors of death
open to those returning home."[62]

At the funeral of his friend King Follett, Joseph Smith
taught that these thoughts can even bring cheerfulness in
times of sorrow. He said, "[Our] relatives and friends are only
separated from their bodies for a short season: their spirits which existed with God have left the tabernacle of clay
only for a little moment, as it were; and they now exist in a

place where they converse together the same as we do on the earth. . . . The expectation of seeing my friends in the morning of the Resurrection cheers my soul and makes me bear up against the evils of life."[63] John Taylor bore a second witness to this knowledge when he said, "While we are mourning the loss of our friends, others are rejoicing to meet them behind the veil."[64]

President Henry B. Eyring shared similar sentiments when he told of what happened the day his mother died:

The afternoon my mother died, we went to the family home from the hospital. We sat quietly in the darkened living room for a while. Dad excused himself and went to his bedroom. He was gone for a few minutes. When he walked back into the living room, there was a smile on his face. He said that he'd been concerned for Mother. During the time he had gathered her things from her hospital room and thanked the staff for being so kind to her, he thought of her going into the spirit world just minutes after her death. He was afraid she would be lonely if there was no one to meet her.

He had gone to his bedroom to ask his Heavenly Father to have someone greet Mildred, his wife and my mother. He said that he had been told in answer to his prayer that his mother had met his sweetheart. I smiled at that too. Grandma Eyring was not very tall. I had a clear picture of her rushing through the crowd, her short legs moving rapidly on her mission to meet my mother. When I saw in my mind my grandmother rushing to my mother, I felt joy for them and a longing to bring my sweetheart and our children to such a reunion.[65]

Mourning with Hope: A Personal Account

Almost twenty years ago, I met the girl who would eventually, through great persuasion on my part, become my wife. I have been forever changed because of her. I have also been blessed to have known and learn from her incredible parents, Rod and Marlene Savage. This is their story:

Rod Savage describes his early years, growing up in Richfield, Utah, as incredibly happy. He has always been, according to his friends and family, "naturally cheerful." It was during this blissful childhood, around age seven, that a significant event occurred that would stay in his memory forever.

Throughout each week Rod would often find himself inside Richfield's local dairy, either there on errands from his parents or to pick up a treat for himself—and often, both. It was during one of these routine visits, that the bell hanging above the entrance rang and Rod turned to see who had come in. To his surprise, it was a girl, about his own age, that he had never truly noticed before. Like Rod, she had lived in Richfield all her life, and they attended the same school, but seeing her today was different. He was, in his words, "struck" by her. He was completely "fascinated." He watched her intently as she perused the penny candy and soda fountain flavors.

His goggling must have been noticeable because his mother asked him why he was "studying that girl." He promptly replied that he was doing no such thing and was ready to leave when she was. He quickly left with his mother, but the impression made by that little girl never left him.

As the years passed, Rod filled his life with his natural loves, hunting and fishing. However, he kept his eye on the little girl year after year, but he rarely spoke to her. He discovered her name was Marlene Baker. As they entered Richfield High School, Rod preferred the fun crowd while Marlene preferred friends who took school more seriously. Rod said, "My friends and I thought school was fun, but all those classes and all that homework kept getting in the way."

In a casual conversation with his school counselor one day late in Rod's junior year, he was asked, "Rod, who are you taking to prom?" "Nobody," Rod said quickly. "I'll probably go hunting." "That's too bad," the counselor replied, "I think every girl deserves to go to prom." That sentiment had never crossed Rod's mind before. "Maybe I should ask someone to prom," he thought. "But who?" It was then he thought of Marlene. He worked up the courage and asked her to prom that evening.

Almost fifty years later, when speaking of their date, Rod said, "That date was so wonderful. She laughed harder than she'd ever laughed in her life and she got me to think more about the importance of school than I ever had in my life. We never went on a date with a different person after that night." Rod and Marlene Savage were sealed in the St. George Temple the summer after they graduated from high school.

Though they tempered each other, Rod and Marlene kept the traits of their youth. She was reserved and careful; he was spontaneous and playful. They were loyal to each other. They were the best of friends. Eventually, they decided their little family needed to grow.

The day they brought their newborn son, Justin, home from the hospital, Rod had an idea. The baby (who was a just a few days old), he said, needed a tour of the home. He took the baby, with Marlene in tow, through a tour of the entire home: the living room (where he told Justin they would have family home evening), the family room (where he told Justin they would watch countless hours of John Wayne movies), the kitchen (where he promised Justin the cookie jar would always be full), and each bedroom, each picture, each faucet, and any other detail Rod could find. Needless to say, it was a long and extensive tour.

"The tour" became a tradition. When Rod and Marlene brought a new baby home (they brought home six total), the entire family would take the baby on a tour of the home. Even new nieces and nephews went on the tour. As the years passed, grandchild after grandchild were taken, with an ever increasing entourage, through the home. While each tour started with everyone present in the home, most would trickle back to other activities and each tour would usually end with Grandpa Rod, Grandma Marlene, and the new baby.

Then, as it always does in this mortal classroom, tragedy struck their home. It had been a visitor before, but perhaps never in such a catastrophic way. Marlene was diagnosed with advanced liver cancer. They fought with faith. They prayed and begged the Lord for an outcome different than those predicted by their doctors. Less than a year later, however, the cancer grew too powerful, and Marlene was placed on hospice care, where she could pass away in the home she loved and surrounded by the family she adored.

This is where I learned personally what it means to mourn with hope. They both remained optimistic and sometimes even cheerful throughout the entire ordeal. They discussed at length, with and without their children present, their plans

Robert Barrett, Christ Teaching in the Spirit World. © *Intellectual Reserve, Inc.*

for the next life. Though heartbroken, Marlene expressed certainty of her soon seeing her mother and father, brother, and other family members. They laughed and cried together as they reminisced and mourned this unwanted change of plan. They faced the last months, then weeks, and then days with grace, humility, and unshakeable faith.

As Marlene approached what the hospice nurses recognized as her last hours, it was decided that Rod should place her in bed for the last time. He stood up and took his place behind her wheelchair and began to slowly make his way to the bedroom with their adult children and some grandchildren following. In the hallway, however, he stopped. He quietly asked the nurse something, and she nodded affirmatively. Rod slowly turned the wheelchair around and softly said to his children and grandchildren with an attempt of quiet cheerfulness, "Let's take Mom on one last tour."

The group made their way toward the living room, where Rod knelt down in front of Marlene and said through visible tears, "Marlene, we are in the family room. . . . forty-seven years of family home evening. . . . How did you put up with all of us? . . . Thank you."

The group moved on to the kitchen and the closest bedrooms, while Rod complimented, thanked, and kissed his bride of almost five decades. The children and grandchildren then held back and allowed Rod and Marlene time alone. After a few minutes, they all made their way into the bedroom, where they all watched this spiritual giant lift his equally spiritual wife and place her in bed, where he would stay with her until she peacefully passed away a few hours later.

As Rod knelt next to the bed where Marlene lay, he thought of his children. This was a significant moment for the entire family. He decided it would be an appropriate time to tell them once again about the day he first saw their mother. He began, "One day, when I was just seven years old, I was in the Richfield dairy . . ."

Mourning with hope means celebrating the time spent in mortality with those we love. It means we look forward with anticipation to joyful reunions, both in the spirit world and in the Resurrection. Mourning with hope means placing all your hope in the power of the Lord Jesus Christ to return you and those you love to your heavenly home. It means acting in faith upon his commandments until you regain the presence and behold the face of your Heavenly Father.

When I leave this frail existence,
When I lay this mortal by,
Father, Mother, may I meet you
In your royal courts on high?
Then at length, when I've completed
All you sent me forth to do,
With your mutual approbation
Let me come and dwell with you.[66]

Notes

1. Andrew F. Ehat and Lyndon W. Cook, *The Words of Joseph Smith: The Contemporary Accounts of the Nauvoo Discourses of the Prophet Joseph* (Salt Lake

City: Bookcraft, 1980), 20 March 1842. See also Wilford Woodruff, "Sabbath Scene in Nauvoo," *Times and Seasons*, 15 April 1842, 751.

2. 1 Corinthians 15:56; Mosiah 16:8; Alma 22:14; Mormon 7:5.

3. 2 Nephi 9:10.

4. Norman Wentworth DeWitt, *Epicurus and His Philosophy* (Minneapolis: University of Minnesota Press, 1964), 182.

5. William H. Gilman and Ralph H. Orth, eds., *The Journals and Miscellaneous Notebooks of Ralph Waldo Emerson*, 16 vols. (Cambridge: Belknap, 1960–82), 8:165.

6. Simon Smith, comment on Betsy Megas, "What Does It Feel Like to Have Your Spouse Die?," Quora.com/What-does-it-feel-like-to-have-your-spouse-die.

7. Anonymous, comment on Megas, "What Does It Feel Like to Have Your Spouse Die?"

8. Paul Kukuca, comment on Megas, "What Does It Feel Like to Have Your Spouse Die?"

9. Anonymous, comment on Megas, "What Does It Feel Like to Have Your Spouse Die?"

10. Lorna W., https://answers.yahoo.com/question/index?qid=20090506 165547AASRWHg.

11. Steele Commager, *The Odes of Horace: A Critical Study* (New Haven: Yale University Press, 1962), 267.

12. Stephen Cave, "The 4 Stories We Tell Ourselves about Death," *TED Talks*, http://www.ted.com/talks/stephen_cave_the_4_stories_we_tell_ourselves_about_death/transcript?language=en.

13. Howard Jacobson, *The Finkler Question* (London: Bloomsbury, 2010), 14.

14. Anne Carson, *Grief Lessons: Four Plays by Euripides* (New York: New York Review Books, 2006), 38.

15. Ariana Eunjung Cha, "Tech Titans' Latest Project: Defy Death," *Washington Post*, 4 April 2015, A1.

16. Susan Jacoby, *Never Say Die: The Myth and Marketing of the New Old Age* (New York: Pantheon Books, 2011), 224.

17. Nina Golgowski, "Ohio Man Buried Riding His 1967 Harley-Davidson Motorcycle in Extra-Large Grave," *New York Daily News*, 31 January 2014.

18. "Pennsylvania Man Buried with his Beloved Corvette," *History Channel*, History.com.

19. Associated Press, "Family Has Unique Viewing at Funeral Home," *ESPN News*, 6 July 2005, http://www.espn.com/nfl/news/story?id=2101713.

20. Evan Bleier, "Family Holds Funeral at Bowling Alley," *UPI*, 2 December 2013, http://www.upi.com/Odd_News/2013/12/02/Family-holds-funeral-at-bowling-alley/5471386003239/.

21. Associated Press, "Dead Man Sends Cards from 'Heaven,'" *NBC News*, 25 December 2007, http://www.nbcnews.com/id/22394223/ns/us_news-weird_news/t/dead-man-sends-cards-heaven/#.WBPR3S0rJaQ.

22. Antony Jay, *Lend Me Your Ears: Oxford Dictionary of Political Quotations* (New York: Oxford University Press, 2010), 70.

23. "Oscar Wilde Wallpaper," *Los Angeles Times*, 2016, http://www.latimes.com/books/jacketcopy/la-et-jc-13-lastminute-gift-ideas-for-readers--008-photo.html.

24. *The Oxford Companion to Philosophy,* ed. Ted Honderich (1995), 610.

25. Françoise Giroud, *Marie Curie: a Life* (New York: Holmes & Meier, 1986), 141.

26. Richard E. Bennett, "Winter Quarters: Church Headquarters, 1846–1848," *Ensign*, September 1997, 49.

27. LaRene Porter Gaunt and Linda Dekker, "Go and Bring Them In," *Ensign*, December 2006, 43.

28. William Shakespeare, *Macbeth*, act 4, scene 3.

29. Job 14:14.

30. Gordon B. Hinckley, "The Empty Tomb Bore Testimony," *Ensign*, May 1988, 65.

31. Joseph F. Smith to Hyrum Smith, 3 November 1915, Joseph F. Smith Papers, Church History Library.

32. Gordon B. Hinckley, "The Women of our Lives," *Ensign*, November 2004, 82.

33. Russell M. Nelson, "Now Is the Time to Prepare," *Ensign*, May 2005, 16.

34. 3 Nephi 9:15–18.

35. 3 Nephi 10:9–10.

36. Jeffrey R. Holland, *Christ and the New Covenant: The Messianic Message of the Book of Mormon* (Salt Lake City: Bookcraft, 1997), 251.

37. Richard E. Bennett, "From Calvary to Cumorah: What Mormon History Means to Me," *Religious Educator* 8, no. 3 (2007): 101–12.

38. G. Stanley Hall, "Thanatophobia and Immortality," *American Journal of Psychology* 26, no. 4 (October 1915): 561.

39. *Teachings of Presidents of the Church: Joseph Smith* (Salt Lake City: The Church of Jesus Christ of Latter-day Saints, 2011), 49.

40. Dieter F. Uchtdorf, "Grateful in Any Circumstances," *Ensign*, May 2014, 76–77.

41. LDS Bible Dictionary, "Miracles."

42. Henry Eyring, *Reflections of a Scientist*, ed. Harden R. Eyring (Salt Lake City: Deseret Book, 1983), 93.

43. 2 Peter 1:16.

44. James E. Talmage, *Jesus the Christ* (Salt Lake City: Deseret Book, 1979), 649, 699.

45. Acts 5:39.

46. F. F. Bruce, *The New Testament Documents: Are They Reliable?* (Grand Rapids, MI: Eerdmans, 1960), 45–46.

47. Bruce, *New Testament Documents*, 10.

48. E. F. Schumacher, *A Guide for the Perplexed* (New York: Harper & Row, 1977), 61.

49. Schumacher, *A Guide for the Perplexed*, 131.

50. Eyring, *Reflections of a Scientist*, 61.

51. Russell M. Nelson, "Life after Life," *Ensign*, May 1987, 10.

52. Mosiah 16:8–9.

53. Eliza R. Snow, "Apostrophe to Death," *Times and Seasons*, 15 December 1842, 48.

54. Daniel K Judd, *The Fortunate Fall: Understanding the Blessings and Burdens of Adversity* (Salt Lake City: Deseret Book, 2011).

55. *Watchwords for the Warfare of Life from Dr. Martin Luther* (New York: M. W. Dodd, 1869), 317.

56. Dieter F. Uchtdorf, "The Gift of Grace," *Ensign*, May 2015, 107–11.

57. Phillips Brooks, *The Spiritual Man and Other Sermons* (London: R. D. Dickinson, 1895), 151–52.

58. Mosiah 16:8; Alma 22:14; Mormon 7:5.

59. Emma Lou Thayne, "Where Can I Turn for Peace?," *Hymns* (Salt Lake City: The Church of Jesus Christ of Latter-day Saints, 1985), no. 129.

60. Edward Behr and Claude-Michel Schönberg, *The Complete Book of Les Misérables* (New York: Arcade, 1989), 28.

61. Thomas S. Monson, "Be of Good Cheer," *Ensign*, May 2009, 92.

62. Russell M. Nelson, "Doors of Death," *Ensign*, May 1992, 72–74.

63. *Teachings of Presidents of the Church: Joseph Smith* (Salt Lake City: The Church of Jesus Christ of Latter-day Saints, 2011), 171–81.

64. John Taylor, in *Journal of Discourses*, 21:177.

65. Henry B. Eyring, "Write upon My Heart," *Ensign*, November 2000, 87.

66. Eliza R. Snow, "O My Father," *Hymns*, no. 292.

INDEX

mourning
  and coping with death, 125–32
  experience of, 124–25
  with hope, 121–22, 145–50

N

Nelson, Dantzel, 131–32
Nelson, Russell M., 131–32
Nephites, Jesus Christ appears to, 132–34

O

obedience, 9, 97, 103, 115, 118
Orlando, Eric, 92–93

P

Page, Larry, 126
participation model of salvation, 64–66
pedicures, 105–6
personal revelation, 38–43, 52n17
Peter, 104–6
pioneers, 129–30
Pond, Maria, 129
Pond, Stillman, 129
prayer(s)
  in Garden of Gethsemane, 11–13, 15
  Intercessory Prayer, 116–19
prophets, bear witness of Christ, 5, 22, 24n7
Protestant Reformation, 89–90
pruning, 111
Prussian woman, trials and faith of, 142–43
purity, moral, 111

Q

questions, asking enlightened, 37–43

R

Rasputin, Grigori, 80–81
reconciliation model of salvation, 64
repentance, 79–84, 111

resentment, 46–47
restitution, 79–80, 85–86
Resurrection, vii–ix
  as affirmation of Christ's divinity and Atonement, 20–22, 28n58
  death swallowed up in, 141
  disbelief in, 137–39
  hope through, 132–35, 139, 141–43
  importance of, 7–8, 51n3, 77–79
  promise of, 140–41
  witnesses of, 22, 136–37
returned missionary, homecoming of, 19–20
revelation, 38–43, 52n17
Roberts, B. H., 40

S

Saint Augustine, 84
salvation. *See also* Atonement; eternal life
  Atonement necessary for, 13–15
  models of, 63–64
Savage, Justin, 146–47
Savage, Marlene, 145–50
Savage, Rod, 145–50
science, 138–39
Scott, Richard G., 37
serpent, brazen, 63
service, 103–9, 120n3
shoes, removing, 120n3
sickness, covered by Atonement, 69–71, 87–90, 91
sin
  covered by Atonement, 64–67
  paying for own, 26n35
  and receiving full blessings of Atonement, 80–84
  restitution for, 85–86
skepticism, 137–39
slaves, 104, 106, 120n3
Smith, James, 127
Smith, Joseph, 32–33, 38, 121
Smith, Joseph F., 30, 131